down to
earth

down to earth

cold-climate gardens & their keepers

Jennifer Heath

Helen McAllister

The information in this book is true and complete to the best of our knowledge. All recommendations are made without guarantee on the part of the authors.

Written, designed, and indexed by Jennifer Heath and Helen McAllister.

Cover and interior photography copyright © Jennifer Heath and Helen McAllister, except photos courtesy of Veronica Robinson: p. 49; Madawna Wiggins: pp. 59, 185; Lloyd Hutchinson: p. 76; Fernie & District Historical Society: p. 96; Margie Sutherland: p. 144; Sophie Ankutowicz: p. 179; Val Rybar: p. 183; David Fuller: back flap (lower); and reproductions from West Coast Seeds seed packet: p. 19 and Plant Hardiness Zones map: p. 26.

Production by Jennifer Heath

Edited by Jennifer Heath and Helen McAllister, with additional proofreading by Bonnie McLardy, content editing by Cait Good, and copy editing by Randal Macnair and Carolyn Nikodym. Technical retouching of cover photo (also shown on p. 21) by Vanessa Croome.

Silk banner artwork (pp. 30, 54, 90, 156) copyright © Helen McAllister.

Library and Archives Canada Cataloguing in Publication

Heath, Jennifer, 1970-, author
        Down to earth : cold-climate gardens & their keepers
/ Jennifer Heath and Helen McAllister.

Includes index.
ISBN 978-0-88982-302-0 (pbk.)

        1. Vegetable gardening--Canada. 2. Urban gardening--Canada.
I. McAllister, Helen, 1972-, author II. Title.

SB453.3.C3H43 2014   635.0971   C2014-905786-5

We gratefully acknowledge the financial support of the Canada Council for the Arts, the British Columbia Arts Council through the BC Ministry of Tourism, Culture, and the Arts, and the Government of Canada through the Canada Book Fund, for our publishing activities.

Published by
Oolichan Books
P.O. Box 2278
Fernie, British Columbia
Canada V0B 1M0

www.oolichan.com

MIX
Paper from responsible sources
FSC® C016245

Printed in Canada by Friesens Printing.

Dedicated to those of you
who are planting seeds

To Dave and Ella, who share my love for the
garden and fully support my passion for growing
our own food. Also, to my parents who planted the
seed in the first place.　　　~ Helen

To the never-ending love and
support of Steve, Mom, Dad, and Lori.
Also to the inspiring folks at Linnaea Farm.
　　　　　　　　　　~ Jen

It always seems impossible until it's done.
　　　　　- Nelson Mandela

contents

INTRODUCTION
OUR SEASONAL STORY

In a climate where there are four definable seasons, gardeners plan their varied activities accordingly. As such, the following pages are set to guide and inspire you on a seasonal basis.

We begin with the winter season. It's a time to design your garden, consider what seeds to order, and enjoy what remains of last season's harvest. As the darkness of winter fades to longer daylight hours, you may even think about starting some seeds indoors. The book then progresses through the freshness of spring and the warmth of summer, culminating in the rewards of a fall harvest.

Within each season there are themes that repeat themselves—like "Viable Crops" and "Enjoying the Harvest"—while other topics are allocated to a particular season.

You will also come across personal stories about gardens and their keepers that are both informative and inspirational. At the end of the book, we have included a short biography of most featured gardeners.

Finally, this book is not intended to be an all-inclusive resource for gardeners choosing to grow their own food. It is instead, a celebration of what is possible in a moderately cold climate. Tucked in between beautiful photos and tasty recipes, you will find a few morsels of information that we have learned along the way. If we inspire you to grow some of your own food, then we will have succeeded.

Enjoy the feast before you!

OUR FEATURED GARDENS

The gardens featured in this book lie in the Elk Valley region located in the southeastern corner of British Columbia, Canada. This area, located in the Southern Rocky Mountains, contains a large variety of growing conditions. On a particular day, it can be snowing in Elkford, windy in Sparwood, raining in Fernie, and hot in Baynes Lake. Within the region, communities vary in elevation from as low as 800 metres to greater than 1300 metres. Frost-free days can vary from 60 to 100 days. Accordingly, we have a wide range of zonal classifications from zones 2b through zone 5a (see pp. 26-27).

Whatever your particular climate, we hope that you will find some information applicable to your own vegetable patch.

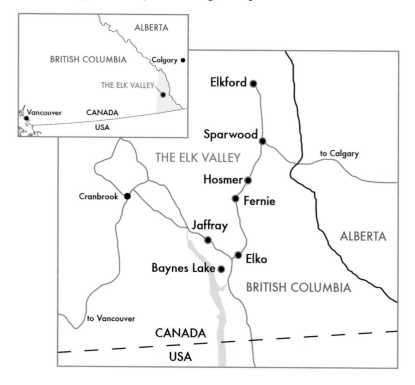

winter

spring

summer

fall

winter

soup   frozen berries

garden planning   storage onions

PICKLED BEANS   SNOW

JAM   SEED CATALOGUES

planning
your
veggie
garden

Long before the snow has melted and the ground thawed, the process of planning a garden should begin. Short daylight hours and the cold outdoors present the perfect opportunity to pore over gardening reference books, sift through seed catalogues, and peruse the Internet for information that will help you design this year's vegetable patch. The possibilities are endless.

• Herma Pozniak's garden dormant in winter and full of promise in the spring. (OPPOSITE & ABOVE)

PLANNING
CONSIDERATIONS

accessibility

Plant the items that need the most attention close to your door, and those things that need a little less love farther away. Also consider frequency of harvest—a herb garden close to the house means you are more likely to use those fresh herbs for cooking.

beneficials

Plants that attract good insects and repel bad ones can be strategically planted throughout the garden. Marigolds, for example, are thought to produce a natural pesticide from their roots.

companion planting

Some plants seem to grow better when planted beside others. Different root depth, nutritional requirements, and insect attraction/repulsion all work together to make some plant groups a good choice.

crop rotation

Do not plant a crop in the same location as last year in order to reduce pests and rotate soil nutrition demands.

days to maturity

This is the time required for a plant to reach maturity and produce food. It is important to understand the length of your growing season when choosing which varieties of vegetables to grow.

growing environment

Soil, water, climate, sun, wind exposure, and shelter are important because they all impact a vegetable plant's ability to grow.

space

Always consider how large a plant will be at full size. Many beginner gardeners cram plants together causing competition between plants for nutrition and water.

seed saving

Decide early on which plants will be eaten and which plants will be saved for seed.

specific locations

Certain plants thrive in specific locations in your garden and barely survive in others. Small variations, known as microclimates, can occur within a garden.

- In early spring, Herma shelters her marigolds from strong winds and creates a microclimate for each plant. (**OPPOSITE TOP**)

- In an I.D.E.A.L. Society greenhouse in Jaffray, gardeners plant tomatoes and basil side by side with great results. (**OPPOSITE MIDDLE**)

- Plant enough peas so that you won't mind saving some for seed. (**OPPOSITE BOTTOM**)

- Gardens will always evolve, but with a good plan, you will be sure to make the most of your space. (**RIGHT**)

SEED
BASICS

heirloom

The term heirloom is used to signify a plant that has been grown for a long period of time or passed down through generations. Heirloom varieties are always open pollinated plants that have been grown for a specific taste, colour, or shape. They may not have the best "ship-ability" or shelf life and therefore are not grown by large agribusinesses. Many growers save seed from these plants, decreasing dependency on seed companies and preserving genetic diversity.

days to maturity

A seed packet will indicate the approximate number of days it will take for a vegetable plant to mature. A pumpkin may need up to 110 days where as a radish may only take 30 days. Use this as a rough guide because the climate where the seed is from may be different from your own.

In cooler climates like the Elk Valley, it is best to choose varieties and species with a shorter number of days to maturity. In Fernie, 70-75 days may be the upper limit for fruit to set on a plant. A gardener in Baynes Lake may have upwards of 90 frost-free days. Methods of extending your season, such as starting seeds indoors, will be required for plants with a high number of days to maturity.

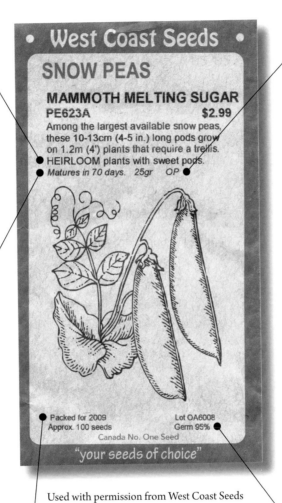

Used with permission from West Coast Seeds

packing date

Check the year that the seed was packaged. Older seed may not be as viable as newer stock. Some seed, like peas, will last for years, while others, like onions and leeks, may not germinate after 2 years.

open pollinated (OP) or hybrid (F1 or F2)

Open pollinated or hybrid refers to the way in which the plant was reproduced. A plant can be only one or the other.

When you see OP on a packet the seed is open pollinated. Two plants or "parents" with the same genetic information are crossed, creating a plant exactly like the parents. Peas, beans, and lettuce are usually open pollinated, making them easy plants to save seed from.

When you see F1 or F2 on a packet the seed is hybridized. It implies the first or second generation of the seed. Two genetically different varieties or "parent" plants are crossed creating a plant or "offspring" with desired traits. This process produces plants with specific characteristics such as colour, disease resistance, or taste. Squash and carrots are often hybrid varieties. These plants are generally harder to save seed from. Hybrid is not to be confused with "genetically modified" (p. 23).

germination rate

Many seed packets will include a germination rate as a percentage, helping you know how many seeds to plant. For example, if the germination rate of a tomato seed is 80% and you would like to end up with eight plants, you would sow 10 seeds.

I.D.E.A.L. SOCIETY
SEEDS OF CHANGE

For the members of the I.D.E.A.L. Society in Jaffray, a good start is very important. That's why they grow up to 85% of all their plants from seed. Natacha Kolesar, the group's founder, explains how each seed is "asked to attract energies to help it grow." Their nourishment of a completely organic environment produces plentiful fruit trees, huge heads of cabbage and lettuce, large beets and abundant herbs, among their many other crops. Starting vegetables from seed allows gardeners to create a growing process based on their own values.

- Several greenhouses and large areas set aside for crop production sustain those living at the I.D.E.A.L. Society farm. They also have surplus food and juice to sell at local farmers' markets. (TOP)

- Daniel and Pierre proudly show the results of all their hard work. (RIGHT)

THE NELSONS
CARROT SEED TRIALS

Experimenting with seed variety is what Terry Nelson does best. Trialling several types of carrots, for example, he enjoys discovering which varieties grow best in his garden, and which are the tastiest. Thanks to ample space, the Nelsons can experiment with many crops, have a few failures, and still have plenty to eat, share, and store at summer's end. If you are limited on space, choose a packet with a blend of varieties to find your future favourite.

WHAT IS A GMO?

A plant that is created in a lab by incorporating genetic material of one plant into another plant is said to have been genetically engineered (GE) or is called a genetically modified organism (GMO). The modified plant may even include material from a completely different organism.

This technology is mostly used to produce seed for food crops that have desirable traits, such as longer shelf life. However, modification is also used to create plants that are resistant to specific herbicides.

No long-term studies have been done on the safety of human consumption of genetically modified foods and companies are not required to label GM ingredients. These companies have even lobbied the American and Canadian governments so that products free from GMOs are not allowed to use "GM-free" labelling.

THE BIG BUSINESS
OF SEED

Seeds are the source of all of our food. In recent years, large agribusiness companies have seen the money-making potential of seed. They have been buying up seed sources worldwide, increasing their control over global agriculture. Monsanto, Dupont, and Syngenta currently own more than half (53%) of the world's commercial seed market. Monsanto itself is the world's largest seed company (controlling 27% of the market) as well as the fourth largest pesticide company.[1]

Due to this market dominance, farmers and gardeners are becoming dependent upon just a handful of seed companies. Many of these businesses sell only their patented seed, limiting the availability of heirloom varieties that have been grown for centuries. This sales approach affects our food supply on a global scale.

Seed diversity is decreasing and our choices are thus becoming limited. In addition, farmers are legally prevented from saving patented seed, disrupting an ancient agricultural practice. Companies profit tremendously from farmers who must buy seed year after year. They also profit from the pesticides and herbicides that work in conjunction with their seed.

Manufacturers are also creating patented seed from GMOs. Of all the canola grown in Canada, 80% is genetically modified.[2] Many foods found in our grocery stores contain canola, soy, and corn grown from this genetically modified seed. Businesses are required to submit a scientific analysis of these foods to Health Canada for approval. Many question the legitimacy of this process, which is based on short-term data provided by the manufacturer itself. Consumers have unknowingly become the guinea pigs for this new technology.

In many countries around the world—including Switzerland, Germany, and New Zealand—people have demanded that their governments ban the production of these products. After Hurricane Katrina destroyed most of Haiti, Monsanto donated 60,000 sacks of seed to farmers, some treated with pesticides. In response, the farmers burned the seed in large demonstrations against the company and their products. Sadly, in North America, many know nothing about the harmful chemicals sometimes used to treat seeds and fewer yet are aware of GMOs.

[1] Who Will Control the Green Economy?, ETC Group, 2011
[2] Canola Council of Canada, www.canolacouncil.org , 2014

TOP 5
WAYS TO LOVE SEEDS

plan to save
Design your garden with seed saving in mind. Wrap a section of peas or beans with bright ribbon to make sure no one picks from those plants. Plan to sow a tomato variety that does well in your region.

purchase non-genetically modified seed
Support only companies that do not knowingly sell genetically modified seed. This information is usually found at the beginning of a seed catalogue.

join a seed-savers exchange
Groups like Seeds of Diversity Canada and The Seed Sanctuary encourage members to save seed and then to share their varieties with a network of gardeners across the country. The seed varieties number into the thousands and ensure that rare heirloom varieties continue to exist.

start a seed swap
Plan a "Seedy Saturday" for your community or friends. Trade seed with other gardeners and hear about what works for them in your specific climate.

process your own seeds
Learn how to process and store all sorts of seeds. Open pollinated plants are the easiest way to start. Challenge yourself with hybrid varieties of squash, which require more technical pollinating methods. See page 19 for seed basics.

SAFE SEED COMPANIES

Keeping on top of which seed companies sell non-genetically modified seeds can be challenging. Things change, companies get bought and sold, and policies may be modified. The only way you can be sure that you are purchasing seed that has not been genetically modified is to ask the seed company itself. Many companies include a note about their commitment to safe seed on their website and in their seed catalogue. Do not be afraid to ask. You are their customer and have the right to know what you are buying, growing, and eating.

There are many excellent Canadian seed companies that are committed to selling vegetable seeds that have not been genetically modified.

Good resource lists can be found on the following websites:
www.seeds.ca (Seeds of Diversity)
www.gefreebc.wordpress.com (Society for a GE Free BC)
www.smallfarmcanada.ca (check their current Seed Buying Guide)

Seed companies vary in size. Most have excellent online and phone-order options available. Get to know your seed sources and find your favourites. Try to buy reputable seed locally, as businesses will supply what people buy. Consumers have the power to make change.

PLANT HARDINESS ZONES

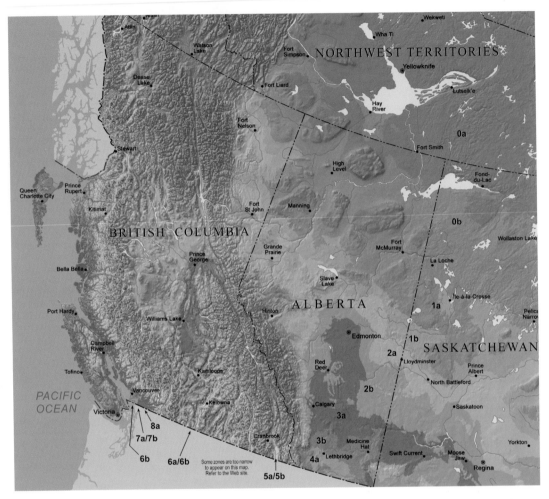

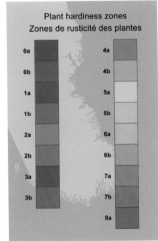

Plant hardiness zones
Zones de rusticité des plantes

0a	4a
0b	4b
1a	5a
1b	5b
2a	6a
2b	6b
3a	7a
3b	7b
	8a

Some zones are too narrow
to appear on this map.
Refer to the Web site.

The plant hardiness map for Canada uses plant survival data and a wide range of climatic variables to determine which zone to assign to an area. Minimum winter temperatures, length of the frost-free period, summer rainfall, maximum temperatures, snow cover, January rainfall, and maximum wind speed are all considered.

The map is divided into nine major zones. The harshest is 0 and the mildest is 8. Each zone is further divided into two parts, with "a" being harsher than "b." Some significant local factors, such as micro-topography, amount of shelter, and subtle variations in snow cover, are too small to be captured on the map. Year-to-year variations in weather and gardening techniques can also have a significant impact on plant survival in any particular location.

Source: Plant Hardiness Zones 2000, Published 2000, Agriculture and Agri-Food Canada, Reproduced with permission from the Minister of Agriculture and Agri-Food Canada.

Plant hardiness zones are used to indicate the general growing conditions of a geographical area. The zones also serve as an invaluable resource to determine under which conditions plants may be expected to survive the winter. Our featured gardens are located in a wide variety of plant hardiness zones, with everything from zone 2 to zone 5 represented.

While understanding plant hardiness zones is less relevant when planting annual vegetables, it can serve as an indicator of what type of growing season you can expect in your area. Generally speaking, the colder zone, the smaller the window of time to allow vegetable plants to reach maturity for crop production. Plant hardiness zones become even more relevant when planning for perennial plants. See page 162 for viable cold-climate options.

Ultimately, the best way to understand what crops are suited to your area is by talking to experienced gardeners. They will know which varieties flourish and when is the best time to plant them. Local knowledge is key to a successful garden.

DAY LENGTH

Your plant hardiness zone is not the only factor to consider when planning a garden. Day length is critical and is determined by latitude. If you want to see how long you can push your gardening season you will need to determine the quantity and quality of sunlight you have.

Most vegetable plants need at least eight hours of direct sun to produce a full crop such as squash, tomato, pepper, and cucumber. Root crops can get away with five to six hours of direct sun, while leafy greens can survive on three to five hours.

MICROCLIMATES

It is also important to choose plants that will take advantage of your garden's microclimates. Subtle differences are created by variations in elevation and aspect, exposure to sun and wind, as well as proximity to bodies of water and urban development. Your garden will be more successful when applying this knowledge.

• The Montmorency cherry is recommended for zones 4 and higher. It grows well in Fernie, rated a zone 4b. (ABOVE)

frost-free period

An understanding of the average annual number of frost-free days is beneficial for garden planning. The frost-free period is considered to be the number of days between the last spring frost and the first autumn frost. In the Elk Valley this averages between 60-100 days with variation created by microclimatic influences.

EARLIEST
PLANTINGS

If you plan on harvesting onions, leeks, winter squash, or tomatoes from your garden this summer, then late winter is a good time to start sowing seeds. Some plants that require a longer growing season can be started indoors as early as March.

The number of growing days for the plant to reach maturity will determine when to start specific crops. As the seedlings grow they can be graduated to successively larger pots until it is time to plant out in the vegetable patch. Other frost-tolerant crops, like spinach and lettuce, can also be started in a greenhouse or cold frame so that you can pick fresh salad greens before your outside plants have even started to germinate.

Whether you have a greenhouse, indoor grow lights, or just a sunny windowsill, plant these seeds well before you've put away your winter coat and boots.

- Make use of an indoor grow light to brighten the short daylight hours of winter. Ralph Stadnichuk harvests fresh salad greens towards the beginning of spring and also gets a head start on his tomatoes. He is thrilled with the advantages of his grow light, and places it very close to the seedlings for the best results. (TOP)

- If you use a plastic cover to warm your seed tray, be sure to remove it once your plants start to emerge. Not enough air flow can cause damping off, a fungus related problem that can kill your seedlings when they are young. (BOTTOM LEFT)

- By mid-February, the gardeners at the I.D.E.A.L. Society farm in Jaffray are already sowing seeds. With the help of a heated greenhouse, seedlings are well on their way come spring. Seed trays full of lettuce, onions, and leeks are inches high long before others have started their garden plans. (BOTTOM RIGHT)

PLANT NOW!

December 21st - March 19th

If you live in a cold climate, you may think there is little point in even thinking about starting vegetable seeds in winter. However, by understanding when you can expect your last spring frost you can calculate roughly when it is time to start certain seeds. The following guide can help you determine what to start and when.

12 WEEKS BEFORE LAST FROST

start indoors

• asparagus (from seed), celery, leeks, onions, peppers

sow under cover (greenhouse, cold frame, or hoophouse)

• arugula, claytonia, lettuce, mâche, oriental greens, spinach

ENJOYING
the harvest

Winter is a time to sit back, relax, and enjoy the fruits of your labour. You can reflect on the successes of your garden, savour the taste of homegrown food, and reap the nourishment of the goods, knowing exactly how and where they were grown. Whether peeling some potatoes to add to dinner, warming a previously prepared soup for lunch, or adding some frozen berries to your breakfast, the sense of accomplishment is a true reward. The taste is beyond compare.

- Ailsa Hebert and her granddaughter Kylee Woodward learn how to preserve their harvest at a canning workshop led by the Fernie Community EcoGarden. (RIGHT)

POPULAR PRESERVES

blanched & frozen

asparagus, beans, beets, broccoli, Brussels sprouts, cauliflower, corn, eggplant, kale, kohlrabi, peas, spinach, summer squash, Swiss chard

canned

asparagus, beans, beets, carrots, corn, peas, peppers, potatoes, squash, tomatoes

prepared foods

chutney, fruit butter, fruit leather, fruit sauce, hot sauce, jam, jelly, juice, pesto, pickles, relish, salsa, sauerkraut, soup mix, syrup, tomato sauce, vinegar

dehydrated

apples, berries, cherries, herbs, hot peppers, kale, plums, tomatoes

frozen

berries, cucumbers, garlic scapes, leeks, rhubarb, roasted peppers, turnips

cold storage

apples, beets, carrots, garlic, onions, parsnips, potatoes, winter squash

Mary's Herbal Vinegars

The pleasure of a summer herb garden is a fleeting thing. One of the most satisfying ways of preserving herbal flavours is to steep them in vinegar. Not limited to herbs, a gardener can also flavour vinegars with fruit, flower petals (such as borage, pictured below), vegetables, and spices.

Use of flavoured vinegars isn't limited to salad dressings. They have many culinary applications, and can be used as a cooling beverage combined with water or sparkling water, as a soothing, restorative tonic, and as a refreshing wash for the skin and hair.

- Mary Cosman

- Begin with the best quality vinegars you can find, selecting red and white wine vinegars, brown rice vinegar, or apple cider vinegar. Cheap wine vinegars are often distilled white vinegar with wine flavouring and colouring added. For best preservation, select vinegars with 5% acid.

- Gather materials fresh, in the morning, after the dew has dried. Gently wash and dry them if they are soiled.

- Use 1 cup of loosely packed fresh herbs or flowers to 2 cups of vinegar. If you must use dried herbs, measure half as much.

- Use ½ to 1 cup of chopped vegetables or fruits to 2 cups of vinegar.

- Place materials in a clean sterilized jar. For herbs and flowers, crush them slightly with a spoon. Pour vinegar over contents and cover jars tightly. Let the mixture steep in a dark place at room temperature.

- Shake jar every couple of days and taste vinegar after a week. If desired, let stand for another one to three weeks, checking the flavour weekly. If a stronger flavour is desired, repeat process with fresh herbs in the vinegar.

- When the flavour is right, strain the vinegar, and pour into sterilized bottles. A sprig of fresh herb can be added for visual effect. Cap bottles tightly and label.

FLAVOUR COMBINATIONS

Experimenting with a variety of herbs, fruits, and vegetables, as well as different types of vinegars, is both challenging and rewarding. Recipes can vary from one to a dozen herbs, but often the simpler combinations are the most pleasant. Popular fruit choices include apples and berries. Vegetables most commonly used are cucumbers (peeled and seeded), sweet and hot peppers, and members of the onion family.

Here are some delicious combinations that you can try:

- Basil, oregano, and black peppercorns in red wine vinegar
- Cucumber, garlic chives, and black peppercorns in apple cider vinegar
- Raspberries and lemon thyme in red wine vinegar
- Saskatoon berries and spearmint in white wine vinegar
- Nasturtium flowers, garlic, and hot red pepper in apple cider vinegar
- Borage and chive flowers in rice vinegar
- Tarragon, a few whole cloves, and garlic in malt vinegar
- Dill, mint, and garlic in white wine vinegar

STORAGE

Store vinegars in a cool, dark place. Unopened, most vinegars will last a year or two, if not longer. Fruit vinegars don't keep quite as long.

When vinegar is more than six months old, taste before using to make sure flavour is still good. Adding some fresh vinegar from time to time can preserve the flavour. Always keep tightly capped. If vinegar has mould floating on its surface, throw it away.

Jen's Applesauce

Every time I make this applesauce it's slightly different. Apple variety greatly affects the taste, so I suggest you use this recipe as a rough guide to create your own unique sauce. Some apples, like Gala, may need less sweetener, while a McIntosh may need more. The key is to taste your apples first and decide.

Maple syrup or honey is the key to turning a simple applesauce into a treat. It is delicious served with vanilla yogurt or ice cream.

- Jennifer Heath

12 apples
1-2 cups of water
2-3 tbsp lemon juice
¼ - ½ cup maple syrup or honey
1 tsp cinnamon
1 tsp allspice (optional)

- Wash, core, and chop apples into small pieces. If the apples are in good shape, I usually do not peel the apples. I like the little bits in my sauce and feel that they add fibre and nutrition. If you prefer a smoother product, peel the apples.
- Toss apple pieces with lemon juice.
- Put 1 cup of water in a large saucepan, then add apples.
- Cook over medium heat and stir constantly. Apples burn easily, so keep stirring!
- Continue stirring until the mixture boils and the apples are softened (about 15-20 minutes).
- Purée apples with a food processor or potato masher until smooth. You may need to add a little more water to reach your desired consistency. Some people like to put their sauce through a sieve to ensure no small bits remain. If you have cored your apples carefully or prefer the bits, then this step is unnecessary.
- Stir in half the maple syrup and spices. Taste and add more of each if required. At this point, I always add more maple syrup.
- Refrigerate, freeze, can, or eat right away.

AMONGST
FRIENDS

One of the wonderful ways to learn about gardening is from neighbours and friends who live in the same growing climate as you do. Whether information is shared over the fence, at a community seed swap, or at the next garden club meeting, there is nothing more valuable than local knowledge. Reference books, websites, and other gardening resources can only go so far in dispensing information. There are always local influences that alter the "recipe" of gardening.

Garden clubs form for a variety of reasons. The clubs serve as a common ground for gardeners of varying ambitions to gather, share expertise, delight over successes, and ponder options for overcoming challenges with gardening.

In Elkford, undeterred by a limited frost-free period and a large local deer population, the Snow-in-Summer Garden Club formed in May 2005. Virginia Seslija reports that the main drive behind the club is to promote environmental stewardship and to show what is possible for cold-climate gardeners. Together they share their love of gardening, while educating each other and the broader community.

To these ends, the club meets monthly, (except July and August), and has an annual membership of $10. The money collected is set aside as a scholarship trust fund available to a local student entering post-secondary education in the field of agriculture, horticulture, or environmental science. Additionally, the club provides annual funds to the local kindergarten classes to put towards seeds and other garden-related learning opportunities. The club members also rallied over several years and set up a fenced community garden that includes numerous plots of varying sizes. Together they are dispelling the myth that, " You can't grow anything in Elkford!"

- The newly constructed Elkford Community Garden.
- The natural beauty of Elkford.
- Deer are a common sight and a challenge to gardeners.
- Barb Filipe shows us her beautiful "Missing Creek" garden during the annual Snow-in-Summer Garden Club tour.
- Members of Snow-in-Summer Garden Club visit the Fernie Community EcoGarden.

(CLOCKWISE FROM TOP LEFT)

spring

tulips **robins** *transplanting*

SEEDLINGS BLOSSOMS

chives sowing RAIN

arugula **crocuses**

here's the dirt on
SOIL

SOIL FERTILITY
THE N-P-K STORY

Soil fertility is a key factor when growing vegetables. The three essential nutrients needed for healthy growth are nitrogen, phosphorus, and potassium. In addition, the elements of calcium, magnesium, and sulphur, as well as the trace elements of iron, manganese, boron, zinc, copper, cobalt, and molybdenum are needed to further aid plant growth.

For soil to be a rich nutrient source for growing, organic fertilizers can be added to the soil to improve plant nutrition and amend soil fertility.

• As the old saying goes, "Feed the soil, not the plant." In Val Rybar's garden, crushed eggshells are added to increase the soil's calcium. Dried eggshells can be crumbled directly into the garden. If you'd rather keep it simple, just toss the shells into the compost pile. (LEFT)

NITROGEN (N)

is essential for all phases of plant growth, particularly the formation of leaves and stems. Some crops such as cabbage, celery, and leeks are heavy feeders and require a continuous supply of nitrogen. Other plants like peas and beans are able to fix nitrogen from the atmosphere using bacteria in swollen nodules on their roots. By leaving the roots of these legumes in the soil, nitrogen will be released and available for future crops.

organic sources

earthworm castings, compost, liquid fish emulsion, composted manure (chicken, cow, sheep, or bat), hoof and horn meal, cottonseed meal, alfalfa meal, blood meal, cover crops (legumes)

PHOSPHORUS (P)

is essential for proper fruiting, flowering, seed formation, and root branching. Phosphorus also increases the rate of crop maturation, builds plant resistance to disease, and strengthens stems.

organic sources

earthworm castings, compost, bone meal, soft phosphate, phosphate rock

POTASSIUM (K)

is essential for regulating water movement in plants, and helps with the production of sugars, starches, and proteins, and assists certain enzyme reactions. Potassium also increases cold-hardiness, especially in root crops.

organic sources

earthworm castings, compost, greensand, crushed granite, rock potash, kelp meal, wood ash

pH SCALE

14 ALKALINE

7 NEUTRAL

0 ACID

TESTING YOUR SOIL

If soil is too acidic or alkaline, plants are unable to use the nutrients in the soil. On the pH scale, 14.0 is alkaline and 1.0 is acidic. Most plants grow best in a slightly acidic to neutral soil (pH of 6.0 - 7.0). This pH scale will give you an idea of the requirements of some common crops.

With crop rotation or limited gardening space, you may not always have perfect growing conditions. With good planning, you can prepare a bed in the fall for optimal planting conditions the following spring. Also, you can work on lowering or raising your soil's acidity in a particular garden bed that contains specific perennial plants like blueberries or asparagus. A variety of home kits are available to check your soil's pH as well as nitrogen, phosphorus, and potassium levels. With your results, you'll be sure to know what amendments your soil requires.

pH 6-8	**asparagus**
pH 6-7	**broccoli**
pH 6-7	**zucchini**
pH 5.5-7.5	**tomatoes**
pH 5.5- 7.5	**carrots**
pH 4.5-6.5	**potatoes**
pH 4.0-5.5	**blueberries**

SOIL FIXES

**lower acidity
(to increase pH)**

dolomite limestone,
bone meal, compost

**raise acidity
(to decrease pH)**

sulphur, pine needles,
oak leaves, sawdust,
peat moss

VERONICA
ABUNDANT RESULTS

A simple soil test to check the pH level and fertility advised Veronica that amendments of peat moss and blood meal were required in her vegetable patch. The dividends are paying off as food production is at an all-time high and the Robinsons can enjoy a varied and abundant harvest of corn, parsnips, leeks, artichokes, broccoli, and kale, to name a few.

THE ART OF COMPOST

Ask gardeners what their secret to a healthy garden is and many will respond, "compost." While the environmental practice of composting helps keep tonnes of matter from our landfills, compost itself is full of nutrients and micro-organisms that are essential to healthy soil. Adding compost to your garden will deliver the nourishment your plants need to grow.

Entire books and courses have been devoted to building a good compost pile. Key factors to consider are size, ingredients, moisture level, and air flow. You also have to ensure your pile does not attract critters—from rodents to bears. Keep in mind that composting is a natural process. As long as you are not in a hurry, bugs, worms, and micro-organisms will get the job done eventually.

tips to get you started

• Home compost piles should be between three to five cubic feet.

• Material should be added using the 50/50 rule. Fifty percent should be "brown" or carbon-rich matter, and the other half should be "green" or nitrogen-rich matter.

• Your compost should be damp like a wrung-out sponge. Too wet or too dry may cause micro-organisms to stop working, or die.

• Oxygen is essential to the process. Aerating your pile by turning it every couple of weeks may help speed up the decomposition.

• Never add meat, fish, dairy, oil, or cooked foods to your pile. It will take longer to break down, will produce an unpleasant smell, and can attract animals.

RALPH

BLACK GOLD

Ralph Stadnichuk's garden shows a prolific display of interplanted flowers and vegetables. What you don't see is the "black gold" beneath the mulch. A wander through his garden reveals the decomposition of plant matter in all its stages. Ralph's diligence at composting allows him to have a constant source of nutrient-rich soil to nourish his plants. By returning the organic matter back to the earth, Ralph and his wife Margaret reap the rewards of his efforts in a bountiful harvest. Ralph uses a mulcher to help speed up this process of decomposition.

LASAGNA GARDENING

If you have a section of lawn that you would rather harvest than mow, lasagna gardening is for you. Also known as "sheet mulching," it is a way to create a thriving garden without having to dig or till. The soil building technique uses layers of organic material such as manure, newspaper, grass clippings, straw, leaves, vegetable and plant waste, and wood chips.

At the bottom of the pile is a thick layer of cardboard or newspaper that blocks out the sunlight and kills the grass or weeds. Next, layers of "green" materials high in nitrogen (vegetable scraps, plant cuttings, cow/sheep manure) and "brown" materials consisting of mostly carbon (straw, newspaper, shredded leaves) are alternated. Similar to composting, this layering system enables the organic materials to break down in place, creating wonderfully rich soil.

This lasagna needs to cook awhile, so it is best prepared the fall prior to your spring planting. While waiting for the soil to be created by the decomposing matter, roots crops like carrots are to be avoided—their roots require mature soil. Like all recipes, feel free to add your own ingredients; just be sure to alternate the green and brown materials.

| STRAW 5"-10" |
| COMPOST 3"-5" |
| LEAVES 5"-10"
Shredded with lawn mower |
| FRESH COW/SHEEP MANURE
3"-5" |
| NEWSPAPER/CARDBOARD
3-4 layers overlapped - no holes for light to enter |
| CUT GRASS & WEEDS |
| GROUND SURFACE |

DAWN
CREATING SOIL

After learning about lasagna gardens, Dawn Deydey decided to build one of her own. With the help of her son Kai, she built a round garden measuring 30 feet in diametre. The following summer, Dawn's large garden provided beans, peas, squash, and calendula, proving the method's effectiveness in creating garden soil. With a variety of organic materials, even a small patch of lawn can be converted into usable garden space.

VERONICA
THE PRANK

It started as a neighbourly prank. Veronica Robinson was advised that snowshoes were the "tool" of choice to avoid compacting the soil when planting out the garden. The neighbour had a great laugh, but Veronica is grateful because her yields are up, the soil is well aerated, and worms are plentiful.

• A picture says a thousand words... obviously the snowshoes worked! (LEFT)

MINIMIZING SOIL COMPACTION

Soil compaction is the physical consolidation of the ground by an applied force. It can reduce aeration, cause poor water drainage, decrease root penetration, limit the availability of plant nutrients, and reduce crop yields by up to 50%.

tread lightly

• Make use of the same path every time you access the garden in a given season, whether for sowing, weeding, or harvesting. Placing wooden planks or mulch on the routine pathways are excellent choices; snowshoes have even proven to be effective for the initial planting phase!

• Consider creating raised beds to prevent foot traffic.

• Avoid stepping on the garden when it is wet.

garden wisely

• Change your garden plan on an annual basis. This minimizes the repetition of rows and allows root crops like carrots to move through your various beds.

• Add organic materials to build soil structure and increase soil strength in the first six to eight inches of the soil.

• Install drip irrigation, which is less compacting than watering by hand or sprinkler.

• Spread mulch on your garden, which minimizes the impact of a hard rain (pp. 120-123).

VIABLE ☑ CROPS

FROST-TOLERANT PLANTS

Here we take a look at vegetables that can tolerate some cold weather once they are established. Because they are fairly hardy, these plants can survive an unexpected frost in late spring or early fall.

Most of these crops can also be planted quite early to help give you a head start. Being able to maximize the length of your growing season will greatly affect how much food your garden can produce. Spreading out your sowing also breaks up the large task into smaller ones.

- Red Russian kale grows very well in cold climates and often survives the wrath of the common cabbage worm. (ABOVE)
- The Rainbow variety of Swiss chard is a colourful addition to Madawna Wiggins' veggie patch. It grows well in cold-climate gardens. Plant a row in the fall and watch it appear early spring. (RIGHT)

- arugula
- beets
- broccoli
- Brussels sprouts
- cabbage
- cauliflower
- carrots
- celery
- claytonia
- endive
- fava beans
- garlic
- kale
- kohlrabi
- leeks
- lettuce
- mâche
- onions
- oriental greens
- parsnips
- peas
- potatoes
- raab
- radishes
- rutabaga
- spinach
- Swiss chard
- turnips

- Kids love to eat purple peas! Gardeners can plant a variety of peas including snow, snap, or shelling peas. This purple-podded snow pea is a culinary novelty.

- You can never plant enough carrots or beets. Limit manure application to minimize forking of your root crops.

- There are so many varieties of lettuce available. From Drunken Woman to Speckled Butterhead, the options are endless.

- Cabbage, broccoli, and cauliflower are from the Brassica family and require protection from cabbage worms. Covering the plants with floating row cover all season long usually does the trick (p. 78).

(FROM LEFT TO RIGHT)

PLANT NOW!

March 20th - June 20th

The spring season is the busiest planting time for most gardeners. When determining which vegetables to start and when, base your timing relative to the last spring frost. The following terms will help you through the spring planting process in a cold climate.

start indoors

Starting certain seeds indoors provides them with enough time to reach maturity in a short growing season. They may also need a warmer temperature to germinate than your outdoor garden can offer. These plants require transplanting.

transplant

Certain seedlings, like tomatoes, benefit from being successively moved into larger containers as they outgrow the smaller ones. Also, when the weather permits, transplanting includes moving plants into their designated spaces in the outdoor garden. These plants require hardening off.

harden off

Hardening off is acclimatizing a seedling that has been growing indoors to the outdoor environment. This is usually done in stages. Start with a couple of hours in shade, then a few more in sun. Progress to a full day outside, and finally, an overnight outside. After these steps, the seedling has been hardened off.

direct sow

Planting seed outdoors is called direct sowing.

START INDOORS

8 weeks before last frost

- broccoli, cabbage, cauliflower, eggplant, kohlrabi, tomatillos, tomatoes

4 weeks before last frost

- Brussels sprouts, summer and winter squash

3 weeks before last frost

- corn, cucumbers, melons

DIRECT SOW OUTDOORS

6 weeks before last frost

- arugula, mâche, peas, spinach

3-4 weeks before last frost

- asparagus (from 1-2 yr. crowns), beets, carrots, claytonia, endive, fava beans, kale, kohlrabi, lettuce, onion sets, oriental greens (mizuna, mustard, pak choi, tat soi), parsnips, potatoes, raab, radishes, rutabaga, Swiss chard, turnips

after last frost

- bush and pole beans

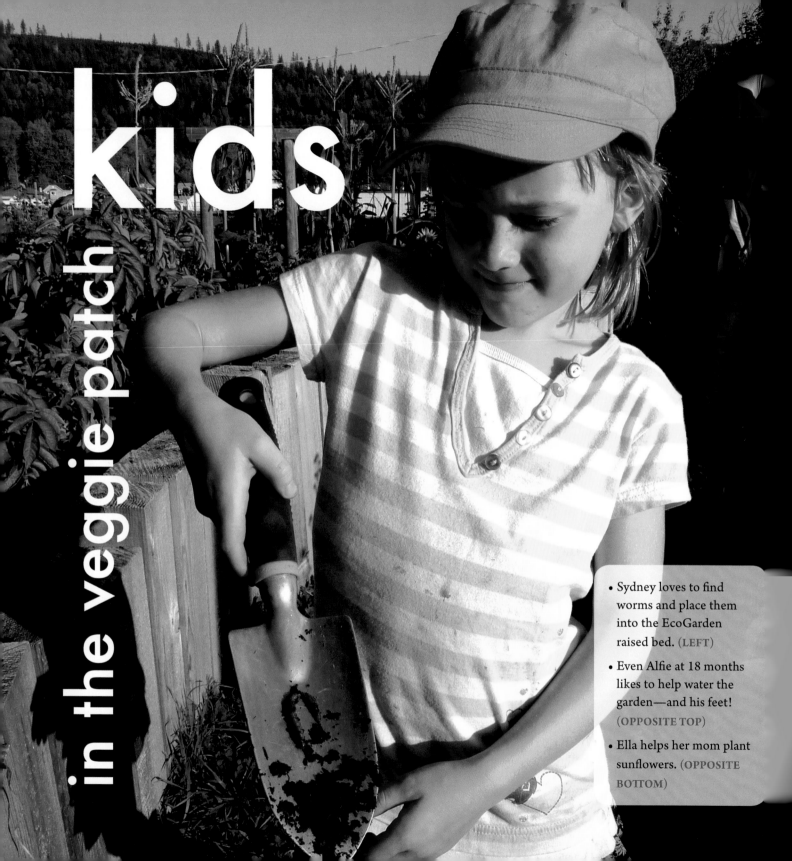

kids

in the veggie patch

- Sydney loves to find worms and place them into the EcoGarden raised bed. (LEFT)

- Even Alfie at 18 months likes to help water the garden—and his feet! (OPPOSITE TOP)

- Ella helps her mom plant sunflowers. (OPPOSITE BOTTOM)

Sowing a few seeds and planting vegetables is a wonderful opportunity for children to learn about gardening, growing food, and enjoying the harvest. Their wonder and joy in watching what they planted grow is very rewarding and infectious. Let them help choose the vegetable seeds, plant and tend the crops together, and enjoy the fresh produce when it's ready to harvest. Pick seeds that are easy to grow, fun to harvest, or both.

TOP CROPS FOR KIDS

sprouts

Grow sprouts indoors all winter long, providing a fun activity as well as a nutritious treat.

sunflowers

Plant these seeds indoors in spring. Kids love to watch these fast growing plants emerge from pots they can paint and decorate. Transplant into the garden in summer—kids will be amazed as their plants grow taller than them.

radishes

This fast growing crop will germinate quickly providing a spicy treat early in your growing season.

peas

Kids love to eat fresh peas. Show older kids how to pick the pods with their thumb and pointer finger without pulling the plant.

carrots

Wash them off with the hose and eat them fresh in the garden. Getting kids to eat their veggies has never been easier.

strawberries

Devote part of your garden to a strawberry patch. Kids love to hunt for them and they provide a healthy snack. They are also easy to pick, giving even the smallest kids a sense of accomplishment in the garden.

FOOD SECURITY

FERNIE COMMUNITY ECOGARDEN
COMMUNITY EDUCATION

The Fernie Community EcoGarden has provided gardening opportunities and community education since 2003. Inspired by permaculture (sustainable) principles, the garden enables members to utilize individual garden plots to grow and harvest flowers and vegetables. They also offer numerous educational opportunities. From the "Farm to School" children's program to "Keeping Food Real" workshops, students learn about organic gardening. Additionally, "Work Party Wednesday" provides volunteers with a chance to learn while they lend a hand.

Community gardens are found in many cities and towns across the country, providing individuals without a yard the opportunity to grow their own food. This is a strong first step to building food security in your region.

WHAT IS FOOD SECURITY?

The World Food Summit of 1996 defined food security as existing "when all people at all times have access to sufficient, safe, nutritious food to maintain a healthy and active life."

The World Health Organization defines three facets of food security: food availability, food access, and food use.

Food availability is having sufficient quantities of food available on a consistent basis. **Food access** is having sufficient resources, both economic and physical, to obtain appropriate foods for a nutritious diet.

Food use is the appropriate use based on knowledge of basic nutrition and care, as well as adequate water and sanitation.

By cultivating a small garden space to grow fruits and vegetables you are working towards improving your own food security.

The Food and Agriculture Organization of the United Nations adds a fourth facet: the stability of the first three dimensions of food security over time.[1]

Food security is a global issue. The scope and ramifications of challenges such as hunger, poverty, the global water crisis, population growth, fossil-fuel dependence, land degradation, and the loss of biodiversity are bewildering. By cultivating a small garden space to grow fruits and vegetables, you are working towards improving your own food security and setting a good example for family, friends, and your broader community.

[1]Food Security FAO Agricultural and Development Economics Division (June 2006)

MADAWNA
TOP OF THE CLASS

Madawna Wiggins is a star student. After attending a Fernie EcoGarden workshop, she continued to research gardening techniques. Ever since, her raised garden beds are a sight to behold. It's surprising to see cabbages, Brussels sprouts, cauliflower, and Swiss chard growing so large in the cool Elkford climate.

By using a variety of methods to extend the season, Madawna has proven that anything is possible. In a place where most would deem the climate too harsh for growing veggies, she has had great success. The short season and grazing deer have not deterred Madawna. She learns the best ways to grow vegetables for her family and improves their food security. Here, she is shown with her typical cauliflower, which could easily provide several meals for her family.

Dawn's Kale Chips

1 part olive oil
1 part Bragg's liquid aminos
½ part lemon juice
½ part nutritional yeast
1 bunch kale

I *love* kale chips. We eat a whole lot of them. In fact, that is the only way we prepare our kale—and we've got over 100 plants!

We make kale chips from baby kale, budding kale flowers, and of course, the regular full size leaves.

Kale is known to be one of the healthiest vegetables around, so eat lots of it. Raw foodists say to never heat your food over 120°F to ensure you maintain the nutrient integrity within the food. We dehydrate our kale chips until they are crispy, light and completely dry. You may find us sneaking into the dehydrator throughout the drying process to eat the kale ('cause it's delicious when it's slightly soggy too).

I love that no cutlery is used in this recipe. All we need is a large stainless steel bowl and our dehydrator. Plus we usually don't measure our ingredients — we just pour until it looks right.

- Dawn Deydey

- Pick, clean, and drain kale leaves.
- Swirl liquid ingredients together in large bowl big enough to fit all the kale.
- Remove kale stems and rip leaves into large bite size pieces (they will shrink while dehydrating so larger pieces are ideal).
- Place ripped kale into bowl and toss with dressing. Let sit a minute or two, then massage dressing into leaves.
- Place kale onto lined dehydrator trays, ideally with pieces not touching.
- Dehydrate for approximately 2 hours until dry and crispy.
- Flip kale occasionally to make it easier to remove them from the trays later.
- When fully dry, remove from dehydrator and enjoy.

Oven method: Preheat your oven to the lowest temperature. Spread the kale out onto baking trays. Watch them very carefully, as each oven is different and kale can take on a burnt taste very quickly. Usually it's 45 minutes at 200°F.

On your deck: Don't have a dehydrator? No problem! Place kale as per recipe on a cookie tray. Place outside on a hot summer day. Protect from bugs with a screen placed over top of the tray. In our experiments, kale chips made this way cook even faster and lighter than the dehydrator.

Storing kale chips: The trickiest part in storing kale chips is protecting them from people eating them all. We sometimes will eat only half a batch and then save the rest in the dehydrator for the next day. If your kale chips last long enough to get limp, just plug the dehydrator back in to crisp them up.

SUCCESSION
PLANTING

Sowing a garden does not have to occur just once a season. By efficiently using your space and being creative with your timing, you can increase crop output and take full advantage of a short growing season.

continuous harvest

To increase your lettuce harvest, sow a row of seed every couple of weeks instead of all at once. The lettuce will mature at different times and will continue to provide fresh greens for a longer period of time.

intercropping

Plant two non-competing crops with different maturity dates side by side to maximize your garden space. A deep rooted plant will use different nutrients in the soil than a short rooted one. Plant fast growing arugula between rows of carrots. By the time the carrots are larger and require more space, the arugula has already been harvested.

one follows the other

Follow a quick-growing spring crop with a heat-loving summer variety. As soon as a cooler season plant like spinach starts to bolt, or go to seed, harvest it all and transplant your broccoli seedlings. After you harvest the broccoli in late summer, plant another row of spinach, which loves the cooler temperatures of early fall. Leave no space bare.

VAL
TRIAL & ERROR

Some people might look at Val's zone 5 vegetable garden and tell her she's got it easy living in Baynes Lake. But Val's yields are thanks to years of trial and error, watching, and learning. By recording on a calendar what she has planted when and where, Val has learned numerous ways to extend her harvest. Val diligently sows a row of lettuce every few weeks (succession sowing) to ensure an ongoing supply of fresh greens. By protecting the plants from snow, her plants can survive down to -10°C. The Rybars eat salad greens until December most years.

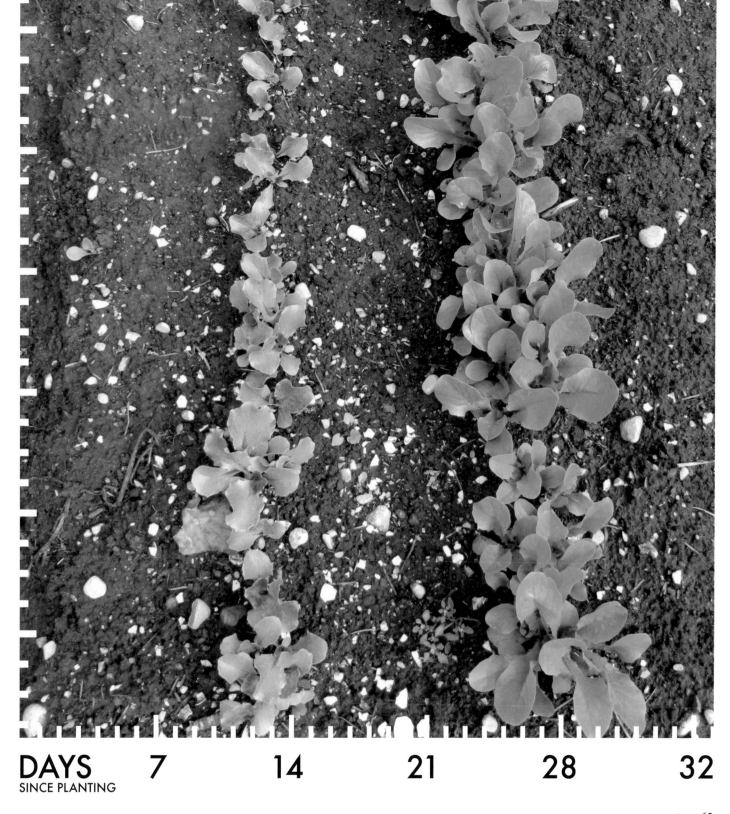

DAYS 7   14   21   28   32
SINCE PLANTING

EXTENDING
THE SEASON

With a short frost-free period there are many techniques gardeners employ in the Elk Valley to extend the vegetable growing season.

In the following pages you will discover simple methods for adding weeks to your season, enabling you to grow crops you never thought possible.

These techniques can be used by anyone who wishes their growing season was just a little longer.

• Madawna uses floating row cover, a hoophouse, and raised beds to show what is possible in zone 2 Elkford. (LEFT)

HOOPHOUSE

Plants that prefer a warmer and more humid environment can be planted in a hoophouse. One can be easily constructed with rebar, pvc pipe, and some plastic sheeting.

A hoophouse serves as a miniature greenhouse and can be placed anywhere in the vegetable patch. Pull back the plastic cover on hot days to avoid burning the plants. Remember to water a hoophouse more than the rest of the veggie patch because it will not receive natural rain.

CLOCHE

Seedlings or small plants that need extra protection from the cold and wind can be covered with a cloche. An old 4L milk jug with the bottom cut out will serve nicely as a temporary warm zone to get your plants off to an earlier start outside. It can also protect your plants from unwanted insect pests. This simple plastic cloche in the Nelson's garden protects a young tomato plant in late spring.

COLD FRAME

A bottomless frame (i.e. wood, old tires, bricks, hay bales) with a transparent cover (i.e. plastic sheet, old window) can serve as a cold frame.

In the spring, it can be a warm place to start seeds, or acclimatize seedling transplants to the sunlight and temperature. In the summer, hot peppers, basil, or pumpkin may enjoy the extra heat. In the fall, you can extend the harvest by covering plants that are still producing to keep them warm and protect them from frost and snow. In the late winter, hardy greens can get an early start providing salad even before it has stopped snowing.

old window cold frame

salad container cloche

juice jug cloche

- Ralph's cold frame gets baby greens off to an early start long before other seeds have been planted. A removable cover can be taken off on those warmer-than-usual spring days. A cold frame is usually a moveable structure that can be placed anywhere in the garden to suit your needs. (OPPOSITE)

- Both homemade cloches and cold frames are used in Jen's low-level, raised bed to protect early plantings. It is important to allow some air flow so that plants do not get scorched if daytime heat increases. (ABOVE)

RAISED BED

Soil raised above the surrounding area can be framed by wood, rock, brick, or concrete to create a raised bed. It can be any dimension or configuration that suits your garden space. When designing a raised bed, consider how you will access the area for planting, weeding, and harvesting.

• At Trinity Lodge in Fernie, residents have the opportunity to grow their own food. The raised beds afford the seniors a more ergonomically friendly design so they can spend more time tending their gardens than an ailing back. (BELOW)

BENEFITS OF RAISED BEDS

extends the season

- Improved spring drainage from snow melt allows the soil to be turned earlier in the season.
- Soil heats up sooner in the spring and remains productive later in fall.
- General heat retention helps crops grow faster and with improved yields.
- Easy to cover and protect in spring and fall from frosts with floating row cover, a cold frame, or a hoophouse.

maximizes soil potential

- Helps with planning for crop rotation because pre-defined areas can be allocated to specific vegetables.
- Added soil depth lends well to root formation.
- Better control over the soil mix, nutrient ratios, and fertilization.
- Yields are reportedly higher and plantings can be closer than conventional rows.
- Soil compaction is minimized.
- Excess moisture through heavy rain periods will drain better.

protection from pests, weeds, & injury

- Chicken wire under the base protects from burrowing animals.
- Netting can be easily added to deter deer and other foragers.
- Floating row cover can be applied to prevent cabbage worms, carrot rust fly, slugs and other pests from damaging crops.
- Weed barrier can be put in place when the raised bed is built to minimize encroachment of grass and other weeds.
- The design is easier on a gardener's body. Built properly, all parts of the raised bed are equally accessible.

GREENHOUSE

Owning a greenhouse is a cold-climate gardener's dream. A visit to a local nursery will show you how advantageous it can be for getting a head start on vegetables and other plants. A greenhouse remains useful throughout the season for crops such as tomatoes, cucumbers, basil, eggplants, peppers, and melons. They require extra work and care, including temperature control, a watering system, pest management, pollination, and soil rotation—but they're worth it!

A greenhouse structure can be made in any size and is usually covered in glass or clear plastic to trap solar energy within the space to aid plant growth. You can purchase a ready-to-assemble kit or design and build your own with recycled and/or new building materials. Understanding ventilation is key to designing a successful greenhouse, otherwise the heat built up on a hot summer day may destroy all your hard work.

A greenhouse can help overcome a short growing season by aiding food production in a controlled growing environment. It is also a wonderful place to soak in the first rays of spring warmth, take shelter from a summer storm, or gain protection from an early fall frost.

- At the I.D.E.A.L. Society farm in Jaffray, the main greenhouse is in full production come mid-summer. (OPPOSITE)

- Glenda Komenac of the Elkford Snow-in-Summer Garden Club proves that even a temporary storage shelter can be transformed into a greenhouse. (RIGHT)

- Jen's greenhouse is filled with tomatoes, cucumbers, and her favourite, hot peppers. Automatic window openers make cooling the greenhouse easier. (OPPOSITE LEFT)

- Helen and Dave constructed their greenhouse out of recycled building materials. At first, friends wondered how they were going to fill such a large space. Now, their salvaged trusses and windows protect a large amount of food including tomatoes, cucumbers, peppers, eggplant, melons, beans, and basil. (OPPOSITE RIGHT)

- Terry and Laura use their greenhouse for starting hardier crops in the early spring and for growing frost-sensitive plants in the summer and fall. (THIS PAGE)

PEP

COMPETITIVE NATURE

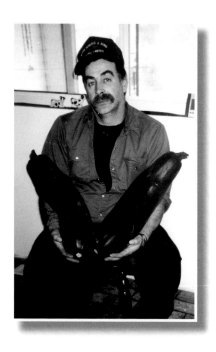

In Hosmer, Lloyd (Pep) and Robin Hutchinson grow prolific cucumber, cherry tomato, and basil plants in their greenhouse. However, crops better suited to the vegetable patch are where Pep devotes most of his energy. There he grows daikon radishes the size of your arm and two-foot long zucchinis.

Gardening competition is fierce amongst the Hutchinson men. Pep has trouble competing with his uncles, Tom and Larry, who try to outdo each other every summer. Within this family of exceptional gardeners, an eight-pound zucchini can still be second best!

FLOATING ROW COVER

Large pieces of lightweight fabric can be draped over your rows of vegetables and secured. The floating row cover keeps in heat and moisture, allowing quicker seed germination in the spring. In addition, it provides shelter from intense sun, strong wind, or frost, and protects your crops from a variety of insect pests. The plants are protected, while sun and rain is still able to filter through the fabric.

Two thicknesses of floating row cover are available. Lighter weight fabric is better suited for insect exclusion. Cabbage, cauliflower, and broccoli appreciate the protection from the notorious cabbage worm, which can ruin an entire summer of growing. Heavier fabric can protect plants down to -5°C. If you are growing tomatoes outside, be watchful for the first frosts of fall. Tomatoes do not tolerate any frost and need protection to prevent irreversible crop damage. Keep an eye on the weather forecast, and if frost is predicted, throw some floating row cover over your plants. Remove once the danger of frost has passed.

ENJOYING the harvest

Although we usually associate harvesting with the summer and fall, a little planning can make your spring full of fresh food. Planting spinach, Swiss chard, kale, oriental greens, or arugula in a greenhouse or cold frame in late winter means you'll be harvesting small salads by the middle of spring.

For seeds that are sown directly into the garden, try quick-growing crops like radishes and greens as soon as the soil is workable. By late spring you'll be enjoying baby green salads topped with diced chives, one of the first perennials available. After a winter of store-bought food, these micro-greens are a treat for your digestive system. Also, don't forget your hardy perennials like asparagus and rhubarb, which bring forth their fresh shoots later in the spring.

quick growers
arugula, parsley, radishes, spinach

baby greens
beet tops, kale, lettuce, mâche, oriental greens, Swiss chard

perennial delights
asparagus, chives, rhubarb, sorrel

BIENNIAL BONUS!

Biennial plants take two years to complete their biological cycle. In the first season, they produce leaves, roots, and stalks. In their second season, the plant flowers and seeds are made. Plants like parsley, kale, carrots, Swiss chard, and onions fall into this category. If you wish to save seed from these plants you will have to leave them in the ground over winter. These plants will be some of the first coming up in the spring. The bonus with kale, parsley, and Swiss chard is that you get to harvest early fresh greens before the plant bolts or goes to seed.

Helen's Arugula Pesto

Arugula, also known as "rocket," is a cold-hardy green that is easy to grow and harvest, matures quickly, and is delicious on its own or a wonderful accompaniment in salads. Baby greens are mild in taste while more mature plants can be quite "picante."

- Helen McAllister

4 cups packed arugula
12 cloves garlic - roasted
1 clove garlic - raw
½ cup of roasted nuts/seeds
  (ideas include: pumpkin seeds, walnuts, pine nuts)
1 cup olive oil

- Pick arugula when it is cool—first thing in the morning or late in the day. Wash thoroughly and dry.
- Roast garlic. The easiest way to do this is to separate the cloves but keep them in their individual skins and place them in a frying pan on the stove on medium heat turning occasionally until roasted (5-10 minutes).
- Roast nuts/seeds. You can choose to roast just one variety of nut or seed or create a mix (whatever you have on hand, or flavour you prefer).
- In a blender, add small amounts of each ingredient and drizzle the olive oil in gradually. Add a little more oil if consistency requires.
- When fully mixed, spoon into ice cube trays and place in freezer. Once completely frozen, place cubes in a freezer bag ready for use whenever you need some delicious pesto.
- Parmesan cheese can also be added to the thawed pesto.
- Note: the same quantities can be used when making basil pesto—simply replace the arugula with basil.

summer

sunflowers growth *mulch*

FARMERS' MARKETS PEAS

SUN berries salads

VIABLE ☑
CROPS

FROST-SENSITIVE PLANTS

Some annual crops are not cold-tolerant and cannot handle a hard frost. They need protection from the cold both early spring and late summer to help fruit reach maturity. Plants like squash will have leaf damage from an unexpected frost, but can recover and continue to grow new leaves. Other plants like tomatoes and basil, will completely die if exposed to a hard frost.

Use floating row cover, a cloche, a cold frame, a hoophouse, or a greenhouse to ensure these tender plants survive. See "frost-free period" on page 27 to understand your frost-free growing season.

- basil

- beans (bush, pole)

- corn

- cucumbers

- eggplant

- melons

- peppers (sweet, hot)

- squash (summer, winter)

- tomatoes

- tomatillos

- Basil is quite sensitive to frost and its leaves will turn black if exposed to a chilly evening without cover. In a small hoophouse (p.66), this aromatic herb pairs well with cucumber plants. Both the upright basil and sprawling cucumber enjoy warm soil and moist air. Don't forget to open the hoophouse on hot days. (ABOVE)

SUMMER VS WINTER SQUASH

When referring to squash, the terms "summer" and "winter" speak to when the fruit is harvested from the plant.

Summer squash is picked throughout the summer. It has edible, thin skin that requires little cooking. Zucchini and patty pans (upper left) are typical examples of summer squash.

Winter squash, on the other hand, is generally harvested at the end of the growing season. It gets its name from the fact that it can be stored and eaten throughout the winter. Its tough skin is often removed before eating. Pumpkin (lower left), spaghetti, acorn, and butternut squash are all considered winter squash.

UNEXPECTED FROST?

If your crops get hit with an unexpected frost there is still a chance that you can save them—if you are up before the sun. Sophie Ankutowicz sprays her garden with the hose at the coldest part of the night usually just before sunrise. Watering plants before they are injured from the frost can save them by raising their internal temperature above freezing. If you slept in and damage has occurred then no amount of watering will help.

- Corn should be started indoors—but only two to three weeks before transplanting into your garden. The roots are very long and may get root bound if started much earlier. Corn germinates with the wind so plant it in a block, zigzag, or circular pattern.

- When planting zucchini keep in mind that a family of four probably does not need more than two plants.

- Helen improves her eggplant yield by gently tapping the stem of the flowers. This disperses the pollen, which promotes fruit production.

- Beans can be sown directly into garden soil but will not germinate if it is cold and wet. Wait until your soil has warmed up and dried out before sowing.

- Most melons will need to be started indoors. With a short growing season, you will be lucky to get a few small fruits. Pick varieties with the shortest number of days to maturity (p.19).

- Start your hot peppers indoors. Harvest ripe peppers regularly to encourage new fruit production.

(CLOCKWISE FROM OPPOSITE)

PLANT NOW!

June 21st - September 22nd

it's not too late

If it's the first week of summer and life has been busy, or you've been away and haven't managed to get any seeds or seedlings into the ground, don't despair. Plant your garden anyway. You will be grateful that you made the last minute effort and be rewarded with home-grown goods that far surpass anything you'll find at the store. Terry Nelson tells a story about the year he wasn't able to plant a garden until July 1st. He said that it was one of his best gardens ever!

If you've already planted your garden but notice sparse germination, it may not be too late to fill in the gaps. Carrot, beet, and bean seeds are all great candidates for re-planting. The heat and day length at this time of year often enable a later sowing to catch up.

mid-summer planting

There is a movement to further extend the growing season by starting seeds again in the middle of summer. These gardeners plan to harvest well into the fall and beyond. In a cold climate we have two possible challenges to this concept: temperature and day length.

Surprisingly, cold climates often have very hot summers. This heat does not allow a seedling to mature and the plant bolts (goes into seed production mode). Some gardeners try to lower the temperature with shade cloth. This may prevent bolting.

The biggest limitation to year-round gardening in cold climate areas like the Elk Valley, is the limited daylight hours. When day length is less than 10 hours, plant growth will actually halt and the plant will go dormant. A crop has to be almost fully mature at this stage of the season. Protecting the plants from the elements then becomes key and harvesting can occur when you are ready.

If you choose to trial a second round of planting, you could possibly extend your harvest well into fall, if not winter. You will need to make use of a cold frame, hoophouse, greenhouse, or floating row cover to help you extend the season in a cold climate.

The complexities of summer planting for a fall and winter garden go beyond the basics of this book. If you would like to trial year-round gardening at northern latitudes, there are some good resources available. In particular, Eliot Coleman's *Four-Season Harvest* and Niki Jabbour's *The Year-Round Vegetable Gardener*.

VAL
LABOUR OF LOVE

For Val Rybar, the vegetable garden is a full-time job and a passion. "Why would I work and pay for food, when I can grow my own and know exactly what I'm eating. [It is] much better than being paid for something I don't want to do." Her vegetable patch and cellar are a testament to her labour of love. With the increasing cost of food, you, too, may find it economical to plant a small garden. Even a few rows of carrots or pots of herbs can save you some hard-earned cash.

MIMI & TREVOR

SUSTAINABLE CIRCLE

Mimi and Trevor are an inspiration to young families. The Nickerson family shows how sustainable gardening practices can be done. On their small parcel of land in Elko, they grow a small vegetable patch and a greenhouse full of tomatoes, eggplants, and basil.

By feeding the vegetable scraps and other plant matter from their land to their flock of chickens, the chickens, in turn, provide the family and their neighbours with a surplus of eggs. The nutrient-rich poultry manure is composted and returned to the vegetable patch to make healthy soil. They are rewarded each year with many vegetables to feed their family and so the cycle repeats itself.

Veronica's
Zucchini Relish & Pickles

GRAND SCALE ZUCCHINI RELISH

Yields: 8 pints

10 cups minced zucchini
1 cup pickling salt
5 cups minced onion
1 cup diced celery
3 green peppers, diced
2 sweet red peppers, diced
2 tsp turmeric
1 tbsp dry mustard
3 tbsp celery seeds
6 cups sugar
5 cups white vinegar
3 tbsp cornstarch

- Combine the zucchini with the salt and the other vegetables. Allow the mixture to stand overnight. Drain, rinse thoroughly and drain again in a colander. Press a bowl down on top of the vegetable mixture to force out as much liquid as possible.

- In a large enamel pot, combine the remaining ingredients; add the vegetables and bring to a rolling boil. Reduce the heat and boil gently for 20 minutes. Ladle the relish into clean, hot pint jars, leaving ½ inch headspace, and seal. Process in a boiling water bath or steam canner for 15 minutes (or as long as is required for your altitude).

ZUCCHINI DILL PICKLES

Yields: 3 quarts

3 quarts zucchini or other summer squash
¼ cup pickling salt
2 ½ cups white vinegar
2 ½ cups water
6 cloves garlic
3 sprigs fresh dill
18 peppercorns
3 grape leaves*

- Cut the squash lengthwise into sticks of appropriate size for canning. Combine the salt, vinegar, and water. Bring to a rolling boil.

- Place 2 garlic cloves in each clean, hot quart jar. Arrange squash sticks in the jars; add the dill and peppercorns, and top with the grape leaves. Pour the hot pickling juice, leaving ¼ inch headspace. Seal and process in a boiling water bath or steam canner for 10 minutes (or as long as is required for your altitude).

* Cold-climate grape varieties such as Valiant, grow well in a sunny location.

Excerpted from *Pickles & Relishes* © by Andrea Chesman, used with permission from Storey Publishing.

A PART OF THE RESIDENTIAL DISTRICT OF FERNIE B.C.

CULTURAL ROOTS

Culture is defined in many ways. Undoubtedly when you think of certain cultures, one of the first things that comes to mind is food. Culinary tastes are impacted by the climate and the crop choices available.

The first immigrants to the Elk Valley included many Europeans from Italian, Polish, Czech, and Slovak backgrounds. Their planting influences are still apparent today. The stories and photographs in the following pages describe how culture has influenced gardening practices. These methods continue to be passed on as successful ways to garden in cold climates.

ROSETTA
ITALIAN INSPIRATION

Thirty years ago when Rosetta Rino moved from southern Italy to Fernie, there was a large Italian population in town. She recalls the Czechs and Italians all planted vegetable gardens back then. To this day, Rosetta continues to plant romano (Italian flat) and fava (broad) beans, not only because of their cultural familiarity but also because they thrive in a cooler climate like that of the Elk Valley.

STAND BY ME

When you pass a vegetable patch with a row of sticks you can assume that the garden keeper has had years of growing experience. They are also most likely descendants from Europe or have been influenced by European gardening culture.

You've probably heard of immigrants coming to the New World with garden seeds sewn into their coats? Well, we've heard about an Italian woman who crossed the ocean with her favourite garden sticks. Every year the sticks provided support to her fava beans and peas. Over time the stick ends rotted and shortened, finally needing replacement.

While trellises and netting often bow under the weight of ripening beans and peas, these sticks remain standing.

SOPHIE & JOHN
FERNIE'S FAMOUS GARDEN

Throughout the growing season, the Ankutowiczs seem to always be one step ahead of other Fernie gardeners. John's Polish heritage and Sophie's local knowledge make for a winning combination.

Their understanding of the local climate and when to plant crops constantly astounds passersby. Fellow gardeners strive to attain similar results. The sight of their potatoes emerging in the spring is an indicator that you are probably already behind schedule. By mid-summer, the garden is incredibly lush.

Remember that local knowledge from experienced gardeners trumps anything that you read.

BROAD VS FAVA
WHAT'S IN A NAME?

"You say broad, I say fava." It all comes down to where your cultural roots lie. Either way, these beans are a wonderful addition to your vegetable garden.

Popular in Mediterranean countries, the beans are eaten freshly shelled, steamed, or fried. Some cultures remove the skin of the bean, while others eat them whole. Favas are low in fat, high in protein, and help reduce blood cholesterol levels.

More tolerant to cold than other bean varieties, the plants enrich the soil with nitrogen making them an excellent cover crop. At the end of a growing season, fava plants also add volume to the compost pile.

FARMERS' MARKETS

Wander through a town on a weekend in the summer season and you might chance upon a farmers' market. Larger cities might have a market that runs daily; warmer climes might offer limited markets year-round.

Along with hand-crafted artisan goods, one of the most sought after items is in-season, locally grown produce. Growing in popularity since the eat-local food movement and zero-mile diet concept, farmers' markets provide the freshest possible option for those who aren't growing their own food.

Benefits include less transportation of produce, less handling requirements, less refrigeration needs, and less time in storage. Farmers retain more profits and community capacity building can result from rural-urban interactions in a mutually rewarding exchange. The positive social engagement that occurs at a market is a feel-good atmosphere for community members and visitors alike to enjoy.

JAFFRAY-BAYNES LAKE MARKET

FERNIE MOUNTAIN MARKET

FERNIE COMMUNITY
ECOGARDEN

GARDEN TO MARKET

When surplus abounds, a community garden can sell its produce at a local farmers' market. The Fernie Community EcoGarden encourages gardeners who have an abundance of produce to bring their vegetables to market and the EcoGarden will sell them on their behalf. This provides a truly local food option for buyers who are interested in eating fresh food and supporting local gardeners.

GUERILLA GARDENING

THE MARTINS

FIGHTING THE GOOD FIGHT

Guerilla gardening is the act of growing a garden on a piece of land that one does not own. The concept began as a way to use neglected land productively. In urban areas, gardeners took over derelict lots in order to grow vegetables. Environmentalists threw "seed bombs" into vacant sites to reclaim the land. Activists also challenged land reform by planting fruit trees on abandoned lots.

One summer, guerilla gardeners Liz and Ben Martin, took over the empty lot behind their house in Fernie. Previously, the land had no purpose except to collect random garbage. With a little hard work, their greenhouse and raised beds made from reclaimed snowboards, provided food and fun for their whole family.

Looking for more growing space? Perhaps there is a guerilla gardening opportunity just around your corner.

BUGS
& BEASTS

Regardless of your climate, every gardener has to deal with pests. While one gardener's challenges may be different from your own, you will serve your plants well by checking them regularly. Using a preventative approach to dealing with pests may help you avoid losing a crop.

Here are a few more common ones and what you can do to defend your patch that you've worked so hard to grow.

Deer-repellent strategies:

- Terry hangs smelly soap in the middle of his vegetable patch. (TOP)

- Herma places whimsical ornaments in her yard that move with the wind. (BOTTOM)

DEER

Gardening in the Elk Valley is no easy feat. The window on warmth is short and frost-free days are a rare commodity. Add limited rays of sunshine, thanks to the towering mountain ranges, and achieving some sort of harvest is success in and of itself. To top it all off, seeing deer in your backyard, front yard, and even on main street is a regular occurrence. If you don't prepare your defence, you can be sure that any tender shoots available are going to be snapped up long before you see the herd.

Along with erecting an 8-foot deer-proof fence or caging your veggie beds in wire or nylon netting, other options that Elk Valley locals have found successful include hanging smelly soap (Coast, Zest, etc.) in a mesh bag, or setting up a motion-activated water-spray device. Others plant deterrents like lavender, basil, marigolds, irises, and calendulas in their garden to turn the deer away. A few opt to hang shiny, reflective objects in their yard that will swing in the breeze and scare off the deer.

Deer are creatures of habit so if you can alter their regular foraging path then you will be more successful at deterring them from entering your yard in the first place. If they become habituated to the deterrent and find an alternate route into your yard, then you too will have to alter your plan of attack. Simply moving the soap, water-spray device, or shiny hanging objects to new places in your yard may suffice.

oh deer!

Herma Pozniak tells a now funny story of her battle with deer. She had exhausted every strategy she knew of to keep deer out of her yard. She came up with the idea of using banger firecrackers to scare them away once and for all. But as the story goes, in the process of lighting the banger, she injured her finger and ended up in hospital requiring stitches and a bandage with follow-up homecare nursing. The deer never got to experience Herma's plan—she only got to experience it herself!

In Elkford, there is an Urban Management Advisory Committee. Since 2011, they have been doing deer counts. A count is performed in the urban areas throughout town, conducted in a one-hour period. Counts have ranged from 75 to 150 deer. That is approximately 15-30 deer per square kilometre! No wonder gardeners have such a challenge keeping these voracious eaters out of their yards. A viable strategy definitely needs to be in place if you are planting a vegetable patch where populations of pests are so great.

GRASSHOPPERS

Some gardeners have reported devastation of their crops from grasshoppers. These insects are extremely destructive and hard to control because they are migratory. While grasshoppers prefer cereals and grasses, they will happily eat vegetation of any kind when hungry. Large scale damage is usually seen in field crops, but on occasion when population levels rise, urban yards can be ravaged as well.

Natural prevention through predators is the first-line approach to take. Attracting birds to your yard can usually keep small numbers of grasshoppers in check. For larger infestations organic controls are available.

grasshopper defence

- Cover plants with a floating row cover.

- Biological controls include nosema locustae, nolo bait, kaolin clay, diatomaceous spray, neem oil, and pesticidal soap. An understanding of the life cycle of the grasshopper and the use of the control method is imperative for effectiveness.

- Handpicking is not recommended. Firstly, this is hard to accomplish; secondly, given the migratory nature of grass-hoppers, you could be effective one day, and then a new group will move into your yard the next.

BURROWING BEASTS
(GROUNDHOGS, RABBITS & VOLES)

Various methods can help repel burrowing animals but very few are foolproof. Research has shown that deterrent plants, putting substances in animal holes, and ultrasonic noise makers are ineffective and provide short-term relief at best. The most effective strategy available is to dig a 3-foot trench around your vegetable patch and sink a wire mesh fence into it.

- A grasshopper makes quick work of vegetable plants. (LEFT)

CABBAGE WORM

What initially appears as a beautiful fluttering display of white in your garden patch is, in fact, the white cabbage butterfly seeking out Brassica crops, like broccoli or cabbage, on which to lay their numerous eggs. The larvae hatch in five to seven days into tiny cabbage worms, which have a voracious appetite and can destroy a plant within days.

cabbage worm protection

• Place a barrier over crops well in advance of the butterflies' arrival to prevent them from laying their eggs in the first place. A floating row cover or screen works well.

• Examine plants daily after the butterflies have appeared. Pick off any cabbage worms and dispose of them.

• BTK (Bacillus thuringiensus var. kurstaki) is a natural pesticide that can be applied to crops to prevent the cabbage worms from destroying the hard-earned fruits of your labour.

SLUGS

Slugs seek out cool and wet environments. Mulch is a habitat in which they thrive. While the benefits of mulch outweigh the presence of beasts, a gardener must be prepared to lose some crop to slugs or set up a system to minimize their presence.

A couple of options include daily handpicking first thing in the morning before the heat of the day sends slugs into hiding. Setting up a trap can also be effective. Place beer in a little container set into the earth, empty daily, and refill until numbers are under control. Many organic controls are also available that pose no harm to children and pets. Val Rybar crushes dried eggshells and scatters them throughout her vegetable patch to good effect. Tidying up your yard of dew-collecting objects, including old wooden boards and plastic sheets, will help keep slugs and other pests, like earwigs, away.

APHIDS

Aphids are one of the most wide-spread and adaptable pests gardeners face. They infest a wide variety of plants and can cause considerable damage. Aphids can weaken a plant, stunt its growth, cause leaves to curl or wilt, and delay fruit or flower production. Just as problematic is the sticky stuff they secrete, which serves as a food source for ants and encourages powdery mildew to form.

aphid control methods

• Look for aphids particularly on new growth. Ants are a good indicator of their presence. Squash aphids or remove infested leaves and dispose of them.

• Maintain air circulation in a greenhouse with a fan.

• A strong blast of water from the hose will sometimes knock the aphids off the plants.

• Use an insecticidal soap or make your own organic spray. Combine one garlic bulb, one small onion, and 1 tsp of cayenne pepper in a blender. Mix into a paste. Stir into 1 quart of water and steep for 1 hour. Strain through a cheesecloth and add 1 tbsp of dish soap.

• Sticky traps are a short-term solution.

DON'T FORGET THESE LOVELIES

Other common pests include ants, earwigs, carrot rust fly, and cutworms. Consult with local gardeners to see how they deal with these pests. The important thing is not to panic if you see that some of your crops have been sampled. Many plants can survive common bugs and may even still produce a crop. It is wise to plant a little more seed than you think you may need in the first place. The old farmer's rhyme about planting, "one for the blackbird, one for the crow, one for the soil, and one to grow," may just have some truth to it.

MARGIE
NATURAL DEFENCES

When Margie Sutherland first started gardening in her mid-20s "the weeds grew faster than the vegetables." Almost 20 years later she fulfilled a dream and graduated from college as a horticulturalist. "I was a triple-A student for the first time in my life!"

Now Margie applies a wealth of knowledge in her work at a commercial garden centre as well as in her home garden. Insecticidal soap is her chosen biological method for controlling aphids and spider mites. She feeds her soil with natural fertilizer and plans to add compost tea to her nourishing regime. She keeps powdery mildew at bay by placing two teaspoons of baking soda and a couple of drops of dish soap in one litre of water. She finds spraying the whole plant as often as needed initially curtails the problem and repeats the process if the fungal disease resurfaces.

echinacea

Flowers

Not just another pretty face in your garden, these plants are essential to a healthy ecosystem and garden. Don't shun them for the practical cabbage or onion, for one cannot survive without the other. Flowers offer many of the following benefits:

attract pollinators

Squashes not setting fruit? Plant more flowers and they'll be full of butterflies and bees. Remember, for bountiful harvests, flowers are essential in order to draw pollinators to the vegetable garden.

provide medicine

Many flowers, including native plants and some we call "weeds," have many medicinal uses. Healing plants that have been used for centuries include arnica, calendula, and comfrey.

offer culinary delights

Some flowers look great as a garnish and can be very tasty. See page 116.

entice beneficial insects

Ground beetles, ladybugs, lacewings, and other helpful insects are attracted to flowers like yarrow, cornflower, alyssum, and echinacea. They feed on common garden pests like aphids, slugs, cutworms, and cabbage worms, reducing damage to your vegetable plants.

repel deer

Marigolds are thought to repel deer with their scent. Fuzzy plants like lavender or prickly flowers like roses are also used to keep away the pests.

clematis

columbine

dahlia

HERMA
LAWNS BE GONE

Herma Pozniak just doesn't see the sense in a lawn. That's why her entire yard is cultivated to grow a variety of vegetables and flowers. Several mass plantings of perennial flowers add a splash of colour, require minimal maintenance, keep the bees happy, and minimize the need for pest control. Herma also adds annual marigolds to the vegetable patch to repel deer. Each year, she lovingly cares for bulb flowers such as gladiolas and dahlias that need to overwinter indoors because of their frost sensitivity.

She has no time for the "idiot box" (television) and instead, spends her time planting, weeding, and harvesting. Herma loves to share with others and visitors never leave her garden empty handed.

PEP
FLOWER POWER

Pep Hutchinson recognizes the importance of flowers in producing a great vegetable garden. At each end of his Hosmer greenhouse, he plants a beautiful Morning Glory. With the doors left open, the flowers attract bees and other pollinating insects. This activity ensures a large cucumber harvest. The flowers also attract other beneficial insects, which keep damaging pests in check and alleviate the need to use pesticides.

delphinium

poppy

yarrow

RALPH

THESE BOOTS ARE MADE FOR GARDENING

Margaret Stadnichuk speaks fondly of her husband's love of gardening. She points out Ralph's old work boots that once served to protect his feet at the mine site. Now they are firmly planted in the ground and grow a fine display of annual calendula. Margaret jokes (in all seriousness) that Ralph works more now as a retiree than ever before, but at least she gets to keep him company while he sows, weeds, mulches, and harvests his garden workspace.

Beneficial flowers can be grown in a wide variety of containers. A drainage hole in the base will ensure that roots never rot.

EDIBLE FLOWERS

Add flowers to your salads, decorate desserts, garnish a main meal, or make infused vinegars and oils. Make your cocktails extra special with flowers frozen into ice cubes. Finish a meal with a homemade tea from garden flowers and herbs.

GOURMET PICKS

chive
This spicy flower can be tossed into salads and stir-fries. Infuse vinegar with chive flowers for a flavourful pink culinary delight.

lavender
Infused as a hot tea, lavender's aromatic and soothing properties help calm the mind.

nasturtium
Add some heat to your salads with this spicy flower. The leaves are just as tasty and even the buds can be made into "false capers."

squash
Impress your friends with stuffed squash flowers. The blossoms are filled with a mixture of cheese and herbs, then battered and fried.

viola
These dainty flowers add a beautiful touch to any dish. For the real foodie, try candied viola flowers.

others
Calendula, borage, lilac, dandelion, chamomile, arugula, apple blossom, thyme, bee balm, sunflower, clover, cornflower, rose, and scarlet runner bean flowers are all safe choices.

SAFETY FIRST
- Don't eat store bought flowers unless you are certain they are edible and organic.
- Know what you are eating! Check which part of the flower is edible before serving.
- Those with allergies may not tolerate flower consumption.
- Never harvest flowers growing by the roadside or train tracks.

nasturtium

cornflower

squash

sunflower

calendula

Susan's
healing
salves

Making herbal preparations from your garden is an enjoyable way to learn about the healing energies of certain plants. Herbal oils and salves are simple to prepare and are likely to become an important part of your home medicine cabinet.

Here is a recipe for herbal oil and salve made from calendula flowers. Calendula, or pot marigold, has many medical and culinary uses. It is a hardy annual that is easy to grow and often reseeds itself. The daisy-like flower has properties that soothe the skin, relieve irritation and promote healing.

- Susan Sim

SUSAN
HEALING WITH FLOWERS

For Susan Sim, making herbal medicine is a joy. She lovingly collects plants from her garden and the forest to prepare teas, salves, tinctures, and oils. What some may see as a weed, she sees as a healing plant. Amongst others, burdock, chickweed, plantain, and arnica (pictured left) all have specific benefits for the body.

Sharing her knowledge is also a pleasure for Susan. For many years she has taught students to create herbal remedies from local plants. Learning from Susan is truly a healing experience.

STEP 1 - MAKING THE CALENDULA OIL

- Pick calendula flowers on a sunny morning after the dew is gone. Spread the flowers on a cookie sheet, put them in a dark place and let them dry for one or two days. Next, chop up the flowers and place them in a small jar. Pint-size canning jars work well.

- Fill the jar with the flowers about ¾ full and add olive oil. Use a knife or chopstick to release any air pockets. Fill the jar completely with the oil making sure the plant material is covered. Cover the top of the jar with a piece of cheesecloth and secure in place with just the outer ring of a canning jar lid. Don't forget to label your jar with the date and contents. Store the jar out of the direct sun. You may want to put a plate under the jar in case any oil spills.

- Every few days check the oil to be sure that the plant material is still completely submerged. As the plant material absorbs the oil, it may be necessary to add more oil. Let the jar sit for four to six weeks.

- Strain out the plant material through a piece of cheesecloth, and bottle the golden calendula oil.

- Store in a cool dark place and if possible, in a brown glass jar. Herbal oils will last for several years especially if protected from heat and light. You may use oils for massage, to relieve dry skin, and promote healing.

STEP 2 - MAKING THE HERBAL SALVE

- For every cup of oil, you will need ¼ cup grated beeswax. Heat the oil and beeswax together in a double boiler over low heat.

- When the beeswax is melted, test the consistency of your salve by putting a spoonful in the freezer. After several minutes, check the hardness of the finished product. To make the salve harder, add more beeswax; to make it softer, add more oil.

- Pour the warm mixture into small glass jars. You may want to add several drops of an essential oil such as lavender for fragrance. Again, store your salve in a cool dark place or in the refrigerator.

- These recipes can be adapted to many other healing herbs. Some that you may want to try are arnica flowers, plantain, chickweed, lemon balm, comfrey, or St. John's wort flowers.

MULCH MUCH?

MOTHER NATURE'S SECRET FOR GREAT GARDENS

WHAT IS MULCH?

Take a walk in the woods and you'll find yourself surrounded by it—leaves, bark chips, pine needles, branches, or other organic matter. These multiple layers are constantly in different stages of decomposition. Underneath all this mulch, we find micro-organisms, worms, and insects that thrive in nutrient-rich, perfectly balanced soil.

WHAT DOES MULCH DO?

less watering
Mulch conserves soil moisture by preventing evaporation. With less evaporation, you won't have to water the garden as much. It also prevents soil erosion during heavy rain.

break it down
All that decomposing matter improves the structure and fertility of the soil. Straw is especially good for slowly adding organic matter to the soil.

keep cool
Layers of mulch keep soil cooler, which is good for plant roots on a hot summer's day.

more worms
Worms love cooler soil and come higher to the surface. They aerate the ground and add valuable nutrients with their castings.

bye-bye weeds
Mulch eliminates bare soil where weeds love to grow. Weed seed that is already in the soil often germinates then dies due to lack of sunlight.

- In Jen's garden both straw and pine branches have specific purposes. (**OPPOSITE**)
- Garlic does not appreciate competition from weeds and therefore thrives with a thick layer of straw mulch. (**RIGHT TOP**)
- Terry uses thick, salvaged cloth as a weed barrier. It gives broccoli seedlings a fighting chance. (**RIGHT BOTTOM**)

4 WAYS
TO USE MULCH

wood chips & sawdust

Mulch paths with wood chips or sawdust to prevent weeds from taking over your paths. Be sure to wear a dust mask when applying the dusty material. Avoid composite and engineered wood products.

bark

Use bark mulch around the base of established perennials to prevent weeds from taking hold. Less weeding means more free time. The mulch also holds in precious moisture, saving you even more time. Most established perennial beds with mulch do not require watering.

straw

Use straw around established vegetable plants to keep soil moist. Straw also prevents soil splashing on your fruits and vegetables, making them less susceptible to rot. The soil benefits from the straw as it slowly decomposes. Do not use hay, which contains many seeds. As the adage goes, "Hay, no way!"

If slugs are prevalent in your area, using straw may not be a good choice. The moist environment with a handy food source enables them to thrive.

pine needles

Use pine needles in your berry patch to increase soil acidity. With pruners, cut off the branches of your Christmas tree and lay them over blueberry, raspberry, or strawberry patches. It doesn't matter if there is snow cover—just lay the branches in the general area. In spring, fallen needles increase the soil's acidity. Later in the summer you can discard the bare branches. This trick helps fresh berries taste even sweeter. See photo on page 120.

OTHER MULCH OPTIONS

cardboard/newspaper

Especially good for lasagna gardening (see page 47) because it kills weeds, then eventually breaks down, allowing plant roots to grow deep into the ground.

grass clippings

Apply between rows of established vegetables. Do not use close to young plants as it is very high in nitrogen and can burn them.

leaves

If applying to veggie beds, run the lawn mower over them first to prevent clumps of wet leaves in your beds. This also helps them gradually break down into the soil.

plastic

Many gardeners place red plastic around their tomatoes to block weeds, increase heat, and aid growth. The red plastic is thought to reflect a beneficial wave length of light upwards towards the plants, stimulating growth.

weed barrier/cloth

The best for blocking weeds in pathways and perennial beds. Pay for the higher quality types and you won't have to weed for years.

ENJOYING
the harvest

In a cold climate, summer is the time when you get to enjoy most of the fresh food from your garden. Crops can be picked fresh and eaten immediately. For best results, avoid harvesting in the heat of the day. Many gardeners put in a great effort to plant, weed, and water their garden. However, they are sometimes not as thorough when it comes to harvesting. By keeping up with the harvest, you won't spoil a lot of produce and will make the job of preserving less onerous come the end of summer. August is often a very busy month as we do not have the luxury of spreading out the harvest into the fall months.

Make a point of looking in the garden before you make a meal and you'll often be surprised at how much food you have. A surplus of arugula can be made into delicious pesto and frozen in cubes. Now is a great time to pick berries, make jam, and freeze extra for the winter. Regular pickings from basil, cilantro, and dill will allow the plants to keep producing leaves rather than flowers and, ultimately, seeds. Garlic scapes can be harvested, and either added to meals or chopped and frozen for later use.

Many people associate the first frost with the start of fall. Remember—summer continues until the third week of September, long after many cold-climate areas have experienced their first frost. Be watchful of impending frost that can easily damage more sensitive crops. They can be protected by being covered at night.

early summer

arugula, baby carrots, baby potatoes, beet tops, claytonia, garlic scapes, green onions, kale, lettuce, mâche, oriental greens, peas, raab, radishes, spinach, Swiss chard

late summer

baby leeks, potatoes, beets, broccoli, bush and pole beans, cabbage, carrots, cauliflower, celery, cherry tomatoes, corn, cucumbers, eggplant, endive, fava beans, garlic, kale, kohlrabi, onions, peas, peppers, summer squash, Swiss chard, tomatillos, turnips

CUT AND COME AGAIN

Many leafy vegetables can provide an ongoing supply of greens. By cropping a plant a couple of inches above the soil, it will regrow new leaves. Simply grasp the tops of the leaves and trim a single plant or cut along a row with scissors or a serrated knife.

This method works best with lettuce, arugula, spinach, and oriental greens. Also try it with kale and Swiss chard. When planting for this method, sow rows of seeds thickly, so mature plants grow close together.

This kind of double harvest can also be done with broccoli. After cutting the main stalk, leave the plant in the ground and it will eventually send out side shoots, which produce small florets. These are great tossed into a salad, soup, or stir-fry.

- A harvest basket at Veronica's displays the classic Elk Valley vegetables—carrots, onions, and beets.
- Be sure to harvest your broccoli florets before they open in the summer heat.
- Terry prepares his onions for storage by hanging them in a covered area. When the roots dry out and the skins "rattle," they are ready to be stored.
- Music and Red Russian are two varieties of hardneck garlic that produce large cloves.

(CLOCKWISE FROM THIS PAGE)

Helen's Beet Hummus

This hummus is a delicious spread on crackers
and sandwiches or served with veggies.

Beetroot is a healthy root crop that grows well in cold climates. In addition to being an excellent source of folate, beet tops can provide an early season harvest option and are a wonderful addition in salads and stir-fries.

- Helen McAllister

1 lb cooked beets
2 tbsp sesame seeds, roasted
1 tbsp hemp hearts
½ tsp salt
2 cloves garlic, raw
2 tsp cumin
3 tbsp lemon juice
1 tbsp olive oil

- Cook whole beets in boiling water until soft. Slip off skins.

- Place all ingredients in a blender and puree to desired consistency.

- Chill prior to serving. It will last up to 3 days in the fridge, and can be frozen for longer storage.

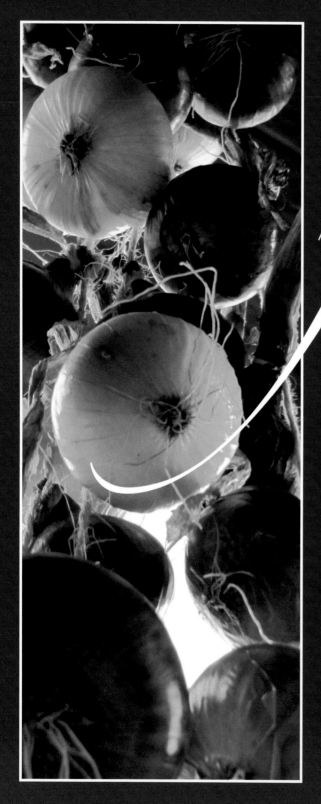

fall

harvest leaves

garlic **tomatoes**

CANNING & PRESERVING

EARLY FROST

seed saving

potatoes

Preserving crops is one of the best ways to ensure your harvest lasts year-round.

STORING CROPS

Half the battle of gardening is to grow healthy plants. The other half is collecting and preserving your harvest with minimal waste. Cold-climate gardeners try to grow enough produce so that there is enough to eat fresh, still leaving plenty to preserve.

There are a variety of ways to store crops. Berries do well in the freezer. Blanching and then freezing is an easy way to preserve kale, Swiss chard, peas, beans, and zucchini. More time-consuming, yet rewarding, is canning. Jams, sauces, and pickles are always welcome in the middle of the winter. Maybe the easiest of all is cold storage. It only requires a cool, dry spot to store crops like potatoes, onions, and apples. See page 33 for an extensive list of popular preserves.

• Freeze blanched peas in a single layer before transferring them to a freezer bag. This allows you to grab a handful or two instead of one large frozen clump. (**OPPOSITE**)

• Air dry your blanched zucchini slices before freezing. Always label items for the freezer, as it is easy for items to become unrecognizable and thus wasted over time. (**ABOVE**)

IDEAL
Cherry Juice
from organically
grown Cherries
www.idealsociety.org

Jams & Jellies

- Using a press makes quick work of an abundant source of apples. Apple juice can be stored in clean milk jugs in the freezer.

- Blanching beans involves placing them in boiling water for 2-3 minutes before immersing in cold water and freezing.

- Fruit juice canned for preservation and storage.

- Veronica's pantry allows her to enjoy her harvest throughout the winter.

- Dried herbs like sage and savory are best stored in a sealed glass jar.

- Grated zucchini can be immediately frozen. Plan to store it in a usable quantity that can be easily added to your favourite meal or baking. When thawing, do not remove excess liquid—add all contents to your recipe.

(CLOCKWISE FROM UPPER LEFT)

HERMA

COLD STORAGE

Through good planning, Herma Pozniak's garden provides food long after it has been harvested. The bulk of her crops include large quantities of onions, potatoes, carrots and garlic. Her storage techniques ensure carrots last well into January, and in May, Herma is eating potatoes harvested the previous year. Smart choices like these allow Herma to continue to eat a zero-mile diet long after the majority have gone to the grocery store to purchase produce from far away.

SOPHIE & JOHN
ENOUGH FOR THE YEAR

The Ankutowiczs certainly know how to get the most from the land they have been tending since 1949. Years ago, John nicknamed Sophie "Miner Jim" for all the rocks she had to dig out of the soil. For all their hard work, they are rewarded with many vegetables to share and store. They freeze carrots and turnip, store onions and potatoes, and can other vegetables that last well into the next season. In fact, Sophie has not had to buy seed potatoes for years. She grows enough each year to feed herself, John, and their adult children, as well as enough to plant the following spring's crop. This is all accomplished on their in-town, double lot.

- The Nelsons harvest several varieties of carrots that last well into April the following year. They wash and dry them thoroughly, cut the tops off, then store them in the fridge in plastic bags or containers. After experimenting with several storage methods, they have found that the fridge works best. (OPPOSITE LEFT)

- When selecting onion seeds or sets, Susan includes a variety that is recommended for storage. (OPPOSITE TOP)

- Herma sorts her potatoes, removing soft, damaged, or diseased ones, then stores them uncleaned in a cool cellar. (OPPOSITE MIDDLE)

- Adding soil or straw around the base of potato plants as they grow (hilling) increases yields. For Helen, a trial of hilling with straw resulted in a surplus of slugs and a smaller harvest. Now she uses recycled tires and hills with soil. The results? Many more potatoes for storage. (OPPOSITE BOTTOM)

- When harvesting her potatoes, Herma is careful not to stick her shovel or fork into the potatoes, as the damage will decrease storage life. (ABOVE)

TOMATOES
THE ULTIMATE PRIZE

CINCOTT FARMS

LEARNING FROM THE PAST

Heirloom vegetables are open-pollinated varieties that have been grown consistently for over 50 years. Heirloom plants are valued for a specific taste, colour, or size.

Over the years, Scott and Cindey Taylor have been growing a wide variety of heirloom tomatoes. They have learned which ones do best in a cold climate and get great satisfaction in providing Elk Valley residents with alternative tomato options. In their greenhouse in Hosmer, they get a head start on the growing season allowing the plants to reach maturity. This provides a wealth of fruit before the short growing season comes to an end.

- Brandywine is a wonderful beefsteak heirloom tomato variety. (LEFT)
- Known for its smoky flavour, Black Krim is a popular heirloom choice. (RIGHT)

VAL
SOURCING SEEDS

A quick glance at Val Rybar's garden tells you she loves tomatoes. A closer look at the plants in her garden shows a wide range of fruit in varying shapes and sizes. Proof is on the tags identifying a diverse array, each plant carefully labelled so that she can keep track of which varieties are most successful. Growing and harvesting tomatoes is a hobby for Val, who sources seeds from as far away as Europe just to see what flavour, colour, and shape she can produce. At the end of the season, she saves seeds from the most prized plants so that they can produce again the following year.

GABRIELLA

GREENHOUSE PRIDE

Against the side of her garage, Gabriella Commisso has erected a greenhouse whose sole purpose is to grow tomatoes. The vining plants grow tall and the fruits are plentiful in her little oasis of warmth. The south-facing aspect is a perfect home for all her plants. She is proud of her produce and rightfully so. Not many in the Elk Valley can boast an abundance of tomatoes—a fruit that thrives in long, hot summers, which cold climates are not renowned for.

MARGIE
INTENSIVE CROPPING

In her small 8- by 10-foot greenhouse, Margie Sutherland packs 17 tomato plants amongst other crops. In order to maximize production, Margie practices what she calls "intensive cropping."

- Pinch out all side shoots that grow between the stem and the branches as the plant grows.
- Once a plant forms two to three sets of blooms, cut off the bottom 12- to 18-inches of leaves. Also cut the remaining leaves by half (see photo) throughout the entire plant, other than the top growth.
- By the beginning of August, pinch off the top growth on big tomato varieties and leave cherry tomatoes alone.

With less foliage, Margie finds she has less pests, less powdery mildew, larger fruits, and a phenomenal ripening process. Her Brandywine tomato is a testament to her success.

ROSETTA
CANNING TOMATOES

Every year Rosetta Rino orders 100 lbs of Roma tomatoes to preserve. She's got the processing down to a fine art.

- Wash the tomatoes and quarter them. Remove the seeds but not the skins. Drain off some of the excess liquid.
- Add a pinch of salt and sugar, as well as a couple of basil leaves, to every litre jar.
- Pack each jar full of tomatoes using the handle end of a wooden spoon.
- Seal and boil each jar in a canner for 20 minutes (adjust time according to your altitude).

Presto. Enough canned tomatoes to sustain her family with sauces and soups for a year.

ENJOYING
the harvest

At the start of fall, the third week of September, the bulk of the harvest in cold climates has already been completed. However, there are still a few crops that can be enjoyed fresh in the fall.

Some plants will benefit from exposure to frost. Their taste will improve and become sweeter. Other crops need to be harvested before frost hits and their texture is destroyed. In a short growing season, they also may not have enough time to reach maturity. These crops should be brought indoors to ripen.

improves with frost

apples, Brussels sprouts, cabbage, carrots, kale, kohlrabi, leeks, parsnips, Swiss chard, turnips

indoor ripening required

melons, tomatoes, winter squash

- Once harvested from the vine, a melon will not continue to mature. Melons should be placed in individual paper bags to ripen.

- In Helen's greenhouse, Red Kuri winter squash (also called Kabocha) is a drought tolerant alternative to pumpkin.

- Fresh apples can be turned into sauce (see page 36), juice, pies, or crumble. If time is an issue, prepare apples as you would for your favourite recipe and store in freezer.

- Green tomatoes can be picked and placed on a single layer of newspaper in a cool, dark place. After a few days to a week, they will begin to turn red. Depending on when they are picked, some tomatoes will just not ripen. After a week or so, the tomatoes that do not show any signs of ripening, probably will not and should be eaten green. Check regularly to avoid spoilage. Many recipes find a use for the unripened gems including the famous "Fried Green Tomatoes." **(CLOCKWISE FROM UPPER LEFT)**

- Try harvesting a few leeks at a time. Those left in the ground continue to sweeten until you are ready to use them. **(RIGHT)**

The Nelson's Tomatillo Salsa Verde

Tomatillos are the most productive plant in my garden. While taking up quite a bit of room, each plant produces about three gallons of fruit. With a unique, difficult to describe taste, they have been referred to as having a lime-tomato-plum flavour. With many uses—including in jams, salsas, pasta sauce, and of course, enchiladas—they are very versatile. The bulk of my harvest ends up as tomatillo salsa, or salsa verde, as is common in the northern regions of Mexico.

- Terry Nelson

Roasting the tomatillos adds a nice effect to the flavour of a salsa. Just cut in half, place cut side down on a cookie sheet and broil five to seven minutes until skins just start to blacken. This adds a bit of a smoky taste. I also like to add garlic to my recipe.

Tomatillos store nicely left in their beautiful husks, either on the counter or in the fridge, but not in a sealed container. They can also be quartered and frozen fresh. As the plants are very productive, we are always challenged to use them all, and so they are great for sharing with friends.

- Laura Nelson

10 cups of parboiled or roasted tomatillos
1 cup finely chopped onion
1 cup finely chopped red pepper (for colour)
1 cup of freshly squeezed lime with all of the pulp
½ cup pickled jalapeño
  (or any hot pepper lightly boiled in vinegar)
½ cup of seasoned vinegar
1 cup of white sugar (or to taste)
1 tbsp of sea salt (or to taste)
Fresh cilantro to taste

- Combine all ingredients and chill before serving.

- For long-term storage: mix all ingredients in a large saucepan and bring to a boil for 2 minutes, ladle into sterilized jars and seal.

- Cumin is a nice addition and changes the salsa colour to a rich reddish-brown.

This recipe makes approximately six quarts. It has been refined over the years, and has had a multitude of variations. Feel free to experiment.

SMALL SPACES
BIG YIELDS

I magine being able to save hundreds of dollars on groceries by growing your own food. With only a small space of your garden allocated to a vegetable patch, a 5- by 20-foot plot will produce more than enough food to feed you and your family for several months of the year. With proper planning, you can grow vegetables that take up little room and yield a lot of produce.

Even if you only have a small space, consider the benefits to both you and the environment of growing your own food. Remember that a front lawn is often a viable option for a vegetable patch. Less grass means less lawn maintenance.

If you are new to gardening, starting small also helps to prevent feeling overwhelmed. Later, you can expand with gained confidence.

TOP TIPS
for maximizing small spaces

sow early
Radishes, spinach, lettuce, and arugula can be sown early in cool weather and mature quickly to get a head start on production.

use vertical space
Making use of vertical space can significantly increase the amount of food you can grow while minimizing the garden footprint. Beans, winter squash, peas, cucumbers, and tomatoes can all be grown in a small space—all you need is a trellis, pole, or string for a little support.

pick regularly
Plants such as Swiss chard and kale keep producing throughout the growing season if picked regularly.

interplant
Plant quick-growing varieties amongst those that take longer to mature. For example, sow lettuce between your broccoli plants. By the time the broccoli needs more space to grow, you have already harvested the lettuce, leaving more space.

preserve the surplus
Learn how to preserve your surplus. When many crops are ready at the same time, it is easy to fall behind on harvesting. Continually harvest what's ready and freeze, can, or dry what you cannot eat. Share your zucchini windfall with another gardener who grows superb basil.

- On a small half lot in Fernie, an entire backyard is devoted to growing vegetables. No need for a lawn mower! (OPPOSITE)
- Scarlet runner beans are a great source of protein and are quite prolific. The pods can be fibrous, so they are best picked when small. (RIGHT)

MARY
CONTAINER GARDENING

Mary Cosman knows how to grow food in small spaces. Lettuce, tomatoes, herbs, Swiss chard, spinach, and peas all grow well in her backyard containers. Across town, at the Community EcoGarden, her 16- by 4-foot raised bed also provides plenty of vegetables. During the winter months, indoor containers provide healthy greens and nutrient rich sprouts. For Mary, you do not need acres of land to grow healthy food—just a small pot of good soil and a little hard work. New to gardening? Start with as many pots as you feel you can manage.

- Virginia from Elkford grows herbs close by the back door—easy picking ensures usage. In permaculture (a sustainable design process), the section of your yard closest to the house is referred to as "zone 1." By placing plants that require regular harvesting close to your door, you are more likely to use them. Crops that seldom need your attention or are only harvested once per growing season—like pumpkin—are placed farther away. (RIGHT)

- Small plots at the Fernie Community EcoGarden are stuffed full of lettuces, peas, beans, and tomatoes. Even in a small garden bed, gardeners are able to supplement their diets with food they have grown themselves. (BELOW)

ROSETTA
A PRODUCTIVE GARDEN

Rosetta Rino's vegetable patch in the heart of downtown Fernie is proof that you don't need a large space to grow your own food. By using her available space efficiently, Rosetta grows crops that her family loves to eat, and that she knows will do well in this cooler climate. She incorporates different techniques including pots, border gardens, a small patch of mixed vegetables, and a home-made greenhouse against her south-facing wall to maximize the productivity of her plants.

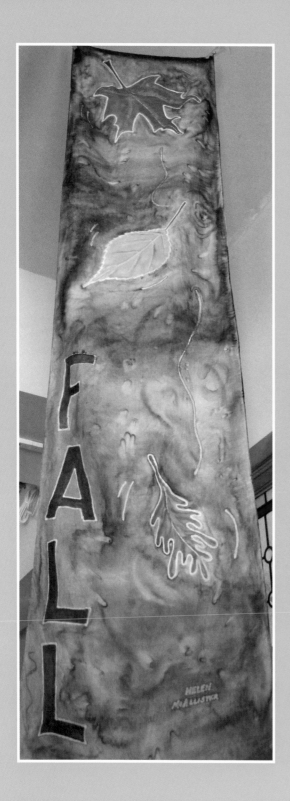

PLANT NOW!

September 23rd - December 20th

In the Elk Valley, fall is usually associated with harvesting, not planting. However, there are several planting duties that are very important for this season.

garlic

Garlic should be planted a couple of weeks after the first frost date. A spring planting will produce limited results in cold climates. See pages 158-161 for detailed information.

cold-hardy crops

Get a kick-start on next year. Experiment with planting crops like Swiss chard or spinach in a greenhouse or under cold frames. When the seeds receive adequate warmth in late winter or very early spring, they will start to grow, producing a very early harvest. We have found that in doing so, we are eating fresh greens at least a month earlier than usual.

perennials

Dividing perennial food crops such as chives, rhubarb, and sorrel helps maintain their health and longevity. Ask a friend if they have any plants that need dividing. Be sure to give new plants plenty of water so that they develop an adequate root system.

This is also a great time to plant perennial flowers, like irises, that will attract pollinating bees and wasps next season.

GROWING
GARLIC

The powerfully flavoured garlic is a treasured crop for cold-climate gardeners. Garlic does not require much attention, is rich in antioxidants, and tastes great. It has both culinary and medical uses.

SEED

Seed garlic is available from general seed companies and specialty farms. Available varieties differ in flavour, shape, and size. Planting garlic from the grocery store is not recommended as it is sometimes treated with a chemical to prevent it from sprouting. Also, by buying your seed from trusted companies, you decrease the odds of importing a garlic-specific disease into your garden. After your first season's harvest, set aside several heads as seed garlic to plant later that fall.

PLANTING

As a general rule, it is best to plant garlic four to six weeks before your ground freezes. In the Elk Valley, September or October usually works depending on the variety grown. It may take you a couple of seasons to get it just right, resulting in large heads of garlic that store well.

Gently break apart each head of garlic leaving as much of the papery skin as possible. Plant each clove (tip up) about two inches deep, 4- to 6-inches apart. Garlic likes fertile soil that drains well, so you may have to add sand, compost, or other amendments before planting. Garlic does not like to spend the winter in water logged soil. Raised beds are a great option because they usually drain well.

Cover your bed with a couple of inches of straw to help insulate the ground and to prevent the cloves from moving around due to frost heaving.

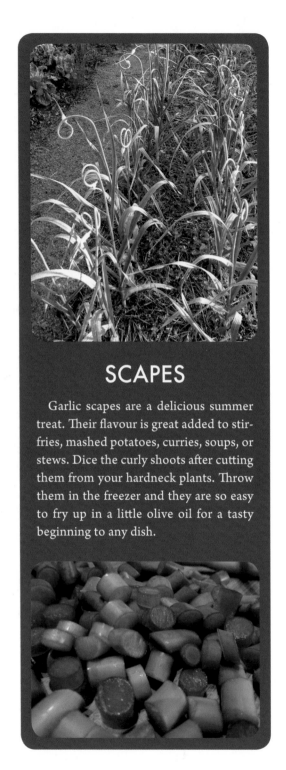

SCAPES

Garlic scapes are a delicious summer treat. Their flavour is great added to stir-fries, mashed potatoes, curries, soups, or stews. Dice the curly shoots after cutting them from your hardneck plants. Throw them in the freezer and they are so easy to fry up in a little olive oil for a tasty beginning to any dish.

MAINTENANCE

Green shoots should begin to poke through the mulch the following early spring. Leave the mulch on, which keeps in moisture and discourages weeds. Garlic doesn't need much attention and with a thick mulch layer, it often does not need to be watered until the heat of summer. Keep an eye on your soil making sure it is moist but not wet.

If you grow hardneck garlic, a curly green shoot called a "scape" will emerge from the top of the plant part way through the summer. Cut them off where they emerge from the top of the plant. Some growers disagree on the actual time at which the scapes should be removed—a general guideline is a week or two after they emerge.

HARVESTING & CURING

A couple of weeks before harvest, stop watering to allow the bulbs to dry out slightly. Harvest when at least half the leaves have turned brown. Depending on your garlic variety, zone, and weather, harvesting times can greatly differ. You may have to alter your timing from year to year and base it on personal observation.

Curing your garlic is also an important step in processing your harvest for storage. Once harvested, hang entire plants in a well ventilated, dry place away from direct sunlight. About a week later, you can cut off the dried roots of the bulb. To clean them up a bit, gently rub until the first dirty layer comes off. Continue hanging for about a week. Cut the stalks off about an inch or two above the bulb. If preferred, braid several plants together and hang.

STORING

First of all, be sure to set aside some large, healthy bulbs of your seed garlic to plant later in the fall. Any damaged bulbs will need to be kept separately and eaten soon. Store the remaining garlic at a stable cool temperature (15-18°C) with good air circulation. They can be stored in paper or mesh bags, or open wicker baskets. Fluctuations in temperature can cause the cloves to sprout and lessen their shelf life.

Garlic is classified as the species Allium sativum. There are also two subspecies within that group—Ophioscorodon, or hardnecked garlic, and Sativum, or softnecked garlic. The mysterious bulbs have been difficult for botanists to classify because shape, size, and flavour are all affected by specific growing conditions. Garlic is "genetically adaptable"—after several years in separate gardens, a variety may look and taste different from the seed garlic it came from.

VIABLE ☑
CROPS

PERENNIAL PLANTS

"Perennial" refers to plants that come back year after year. When choosing perennials, make sure that they will survive in your plant hardiness zone (see page 26). For example, if you live in zone 3, be sure to plant perennials that are rated for your zone or colder (zone 0-3).

Here we introduce perennial crops because the fall is a great time to plant them. Garden centres often have sales at this time of year, and the cooler days allow plants to acclimatize to their new setting. It is also the perfect time to divide your own perennials and share with a neighbour.

- asparagus

- fruits:
  apples, cherries, grapes, pears, plums, raspberries, Saskatoon berries, strawberries

- herbs:
  chives, lavender, lemon balm, lovage, marjoram, mint, oregano, sage, sorrel, thyme, winter savory

- rhubarb

- walking onions

- Sorrel is a sour, lemon-flavoured perennial that is a wonderful addition to salads, stir-fries, or soups. (ABOVE)

- When choosing fruit trees, inquire about pollination requirements to ensure flowers set fruit. Some trees can produce fruit with only one specimen, while others need at least two. (OPPOSITE)

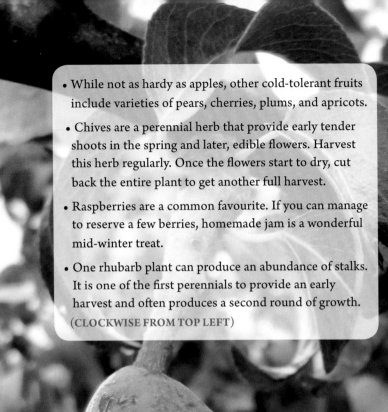

- While not as hardy as apples, other cold-tolerant fruits include varieties of pears, cherries, plums, and apricots.

- Chives are a perennial herb that provide early tender shoots in the spring and later, edible flowers. Harvest this herb regularly. Once the flowers start to dry, cut back the entire plant to get another full harvest.

- Raspberries are a common favourite. If you can manage to reserve a few berries, homemade jam is a wonderful mid-winter treat.

- One rhubarb plant can produce an abundance of stalks. It is one of the first perennials to provide an early harvest and often produces a second round of growth.

(CLOCKWISE FROM TOP LEFT)

SUSAN

PERENNIAL GOODNESS

Susan Sim loves Saskatoon berries. Her property on the outskirts of Fernie is a haven for the hearty deciduous shrub. Rich in antioxidants, the Saskatoon has white flowers in the spring and purple, sweet fruit in the summer. Susan eats the nutrient rich berries raw, freezes others, and also makes preserves.

Always keen to increase her berry harvest, she "sheet mulched" (see page 47) a large area of her property into which even more Saskatoon shrubs have been planted. Because this berry is native to this area, she can be sure that it will grow well and produce a prolific crop.

Identifying edible native plants in your area is a great way to ensure that it is hardy to your particular plant hardiness zone.

SAVING SEED

S ince the Stone Age, farmers have saved seed from their harvests to be replanted the following spring. This process has a multitude of benefits. Saving seed is economical and gives a grower independence from purchasing seed. Saving seed from successful plants also ensures that well-adapted crops will continue to thrive in a specific location. When regions maintain a diverse gene pool, plants are more likely to survive when confronted with drought, disease, and pests. Natural genetic diversity increases crop choice world wide and lessens dependence on pesticides, synthetic fertilizers, and multi-national seed companies.

Historically, saving seed has been an integral part of gardening—no less important than composting or weeding. With global commerce making seed more widely available, many have forgotten the art of seed saving.

In our backyard strolls, we were thrilled to find so many Elk Valley gardeners saving seed. Many cited the above reasons—others said it is just "plain fun." We couldn't agree more. There is nothing more rewarding than harvesting a tomato from a plant that you grew, from a seed that you saved from the plant that you grew last season.

And so the cycle continues...

• At the I.D.E.A.L. Society farm, plants are specifically reserved for seed saving. Here, an onion plant blooms in its second year of growth in preparation for seed formation. (OPPOSITE)

MARY

SAVING SEEDS

Mary Cosman knows the importance of seed saving. Each season, she collects various seeds including those from pea, bean, lettuce, and flower plants. Keeping seed from healthy plants ensures that Mary will be sowing varieties that grow well in local conditions. Also, by not depending on the limited varieties from large seed companies, she is "promoting the genetic diversity and security in our food system." The following spring she will share these seeds and her knowledge with other gardeners at the annual Fernie Seedy Saturday seed swap.

Observing the natural progression of your crops is the first step in seed saving. As plants near the end of their life cycle, fruit and flowers gradually turn to seed.

- As a biennial, the carrot plant will go to seed in its second year of growth, providing thousands of seeds as well as a gorgeous flower. Ensure the wildflower Queen Anne's lace is not growing nearby as it can cross-pollinate with carrot, making your seed non-viable.

- When cilantro goes to seed, it becomes coriander, a fragrant spice used in curries. Cook with some and save the rest for next season's sowing of cilantro.

- Peas slowly dry on the vine and plump pods eventually turn brown and hard.

- The leaves of the lettuce plant taste bitter as it starts to bolt or produce seed. The stems elongate and look nothing like the lush plants that you harvested from in summer.

(**OPPOSITE CLOCKWISE FROM UPPER LEFT**)

aving your own seed can add a rewarding new dimension to gardening. Start with open pollinated plants (see page 19) such as pea, bean, tomato, lettuce, or pepper plants. Once you get the basics, you can experiment with plants that require more complicated seed-saving techniques. Some plants require little more than good timing—harvesting the seed before the fall rain—and a dry place to hang your plants.

SAVING PEA & BEAN SEED

1. Mark a couple of plants with bright tape or ribbon. Tell everyone in your household not to pick from these few plants.
2. Take normal care of these plants with regular watering and weeding.
3. As the plants mature, the pods will turn brown and dry on the plants.
4. Harvest dry pods and lay them out on screens to dry for a week in the shade.
5. Remove the seeds from the pods and save only the plump, dry, hard ones.
6. Store in paper envelopes in a dry, cool place. Remember to label your seeds.

SAVING TOMATO SEED

1. Harvest a couple of tomatoes from a successful open pollinated plant.
2. Scoop out the seedy "goo" and place it in a sealed jar with a tablespoon of water for about five days.
3. A light mould will form breaking down the gelatinous protective seal on each seed.
4. Gently rinse the seeds clean.
5. Dry the seeds completely on a plate or coffee filter.
6. Store in paper envelopes in a dry, cool place. Remember to label your seeds.

- Hang spinach plants in a dry location until you get a chance to strip the seeds from the stems. (**OPPOSITE**)

- Harvest flax plants before the seed pods begin to pop open and spill the seeds. Hang the plants to dry, then lightly break apart the pods to release the seeds for eating or planting. (**RIGHT TOP**)

- One kale plant can produce enough seed for a neighbourhood. (**RIGHT MIDDLE**)

- Saving pea seed is easy. Keep varieties of pods separate so that you know which are shelling, snow, or snap peas. (**RIGHT BOTTOM**)

BIENNIAL SEED

As mentioned on page 81, biennial plants such as kale, Swiss chard, onion, and carrot, will go to seed in the second year of their life. The trick is to allow the seed to mature long enough on the plant so that it is dry and hard. Collecting seed is as easy as tipping the plant into a bucket and gently shaking it until the seeds and/ or pods come off.

Next, you'll need to clean the seed by removing the chaff (dry leaves and stems). This process, called "winnowing," can be done by pouring the seed and chaff from one bucket to another on a breezy day. The heavier seed will drop into the bucket while the lighter bits of dried plant matter will blow away in the breeze.

TOOL TIME

Where would a gardener be without tools? Ask any gardener and they will probably tell you their favourite gardening tool and suggest that you can't possibly garden effectively or efficiently without a particular implement.

The reality is that a simple few will suffice and over the years you can expand your collection to find your own favourites. Here are some things to keep in mind:

spend more initially

Choose quality over quantity. The initial investment will return dividends over years as opposed to having to replace the tool yearly. A tool that lasts a lifetime is gentler on the planet too.

size matters

Think about the size of your garden space. Container gardening requires a different set of tools than a large vegetable patch.

varied uses

If you consider the varied processes of digging, planting, weeding, watering, pruning, hauling, harvesting, and clean-up, you will cover your tool needs.

take care

Fall is a good time to clean, oil, and sharpen your tools. Store them in a dry place. Having a designated place for them is always helpful when you are trying to find the one you're looking for the following spring.

- Dawn has collected a variety of tools over the years. She marks her favourites with her name so that they are easily identifiable whether she is gardening at home, or at the local community garden. (OPPOSITE)

- A decent wheelbarrow can serve many purposes, from moving soil to carrying weeds. Choose one that fits your body size—a small way to help protect your body from injury.

- Proper garden tools can make a tedious job such as weeding more pleasurable. Increased efficiency and improved body mechanics are two advantages Terry appreciates when weeding his vegetable patch with a long-handled swoe.

- Jen uses a bulb planter for planting her garlic. Half the green shaft is approximately the depth that each bulb is sown, and the length of the entire shaft is the distance between bulbs. Find what works for you and stick to it. (ABOVE FROM LEFT TO RIGHT)

PUTTING THE GARDEN TO BED

After a hectic summer and busy fall harvest, there is something very relieving about putting your garden to bed for the winter. Preparing your garden for the winter will benefit your soil, protect your plants, and help make a smooth transition back into gardening in the spring.

clean your veggie beds

Begin by cleaning up the garden. Remove dead plants and debris that may harbour insects and disease over the winter. Dispose of any diseased plant material from tomato or potato plants in the trash, not your compost.

soil building and mulching

Lightly work finished compost or manure into your veggie garden and top dress around perennials. Add a layer of straw mulch on top of the soil to help protect important nutrients from leaching out during the winter. This layer also helps build soil fertility—through slow decomposition—while protecting the soil from drastic temperature changes. If you use leaves as mulch, be sure to run the lawn mower over them first, to help with the decomposition. If not, a soggy layer forms, and blocks out air.

evaluate your garden design

Review your successes and failures of this season. Make notes or draw garden maps, highlighting improvements for next year. You'll be surprised how much you forget over the long winter!

- A raspberry cane produces leaves in its first year and berries in its second. After the cane has produced a crop, it dies. (LEFT)
- Jen's garden gets a thick layer of straw and shredded leaves for the approaching winter. (OPPOSITE)

perennial care

Raspberries: Do not cut back spent raspberry canes. Loosely tie them together with this season's new canes. This helps protect the canes that provide next year's berries from breaking off in snow drifts and ice. Cut the old, dry canes back to their base in the spring, once the snow has melted.

Vegetable and Herbs: Cut back dead foliage on herbs and rhubarb. Put shredded leaves around blueberry and grape plants as well as on your asparagus bed, to protect them over winter.

Fruit Trees: This is a great time to prune your cherry, apple, pear, or plum tree. Compost fallen fruit.

Flowers: Fall is a great time to rearrange or divide perennials that have finished flowering completely. Division maintains the health and vitality of roots and helps plants produce healthy blooms in the coming seasons. Cut back most perennials 6- to 8-inches above ground to keep your garden looking tidy.

For "winter interest" some plants look great without cutting. The seed heads of echinacea, sunflower, and ornamental grasses provide food for birds and shelter for beneficial insects.

A GUIDE TO THE KEEPERS

Here are the stories of some of the amazing gardeners who offered us advice, photo-opportunities, produce, and plants. Their passion for gardening encouraged us to create this book, and to continue to learn more about gardening in a challenging environment. Their love for growing their own food was both informative and infectious.

Here is a glimpse at what got them started and what keeps them going.

SOPHIE
ANKUTOWICZ

Sophie was born and raised in Fernie in the Great Northern Railway House. As a child, Sophie remembers her parents having a garden, but she wasn't obliged to help with it. She married John Ankutowicz in 1949 and together they started their first garden. She recalls, "I was in charge of the flowers and John took care of the vegetables." Back then, she reports, "everybody had a garden in Fernie. Everybody grew food. It's just what you did." John grew up in Poland where everyone owned a small plot of land. Everyone was poor and grew the basics—cabbages and potatoes. "That's how you survived."

With years of experience behind her, Sophie says her favourite part of gardening is when everything has sprouted. Her most cherished crop to harvest is her lettuce. She says "you can harvest it early and it tastes so much better than what you can buy."

Sophie's greatest challenge is when it rains. She finds it gets too muddy to get into the garden and she ends up getting behind with the chores.

sophie's tip

"Start your garden early! We have a very short growing season. You can start it earlier than you think. I am often surprised that I am the only one with things sprouting."

More from Sophie: pp. 87, 99, 137

MARY
COSMAN

Mary was born in the Cuyahoga River Valley of northeastern Ohio, USA. Her mother was an avid gardener, tending flowering plants in her huge yard. Her older brother became interested in growing vegetables in his early teens, and remains an active gardener as a senior.

Mary first started growing vegetables in 1971. She cleaned out and planted a long-abandoned vegetable garden in the Coquihalla Valley 15 years after the rail line had been pulled up and people had long since moved away. She recalls "the soil was rocky and poor, and my only gardening reference was articles in a few issues of *Mother Earth News*." From that first patch with pitiful yields in a narrow valley with little sunshine she committed to starting a garden wherever she lived, learning along the way.

Mary moved to the Elk Valley in 2005. The cold climate of the region has been her greatest challenge in the garden. She really likes getting her hands in the soil and digging the dirt. But harvesting and seed saving are her favourite parts of the gardening cycle.

Mary's favourite vegetable to grow is peas. "They need little in soil amendments, and give back to the soil. They grow vigorously and thrive in a cold climate." She also loves their versatility—edible podded, fresh shelled, or dried for winter soup. Mary continues "they are easy to harvest, to preserve by freezing or drying, or to save seed." She concludes that fresh home-grown peas simply taste great.

mary's tip
"Never give up."

More from Mary: pp. 34-35, 152, 170

DAWN DEYDEY

Born in Calgary, Alberta, Dawn grew up around the mountains, rivers, and ski hills in the Alberta Foothills. As a child, she gardened with her mom. Since 2000, Dawn has lived in the Elk Valley. She references two knowledge sources for growing food. "I loved to walk up and down the back alleys, peeking over the fences of all the amazing old Italian gardens in Fernie. I also learned a whole lot from the West Coast Seed catalog—it's an incredible resource."

Dawn's passion for growing her own food stems from the constant learning curve. "No matter if you are a new gardener or someone who has been doing it for 40 years, you are always learning." Her greatest challenge is taming her passion so that she doesn't let her ideas get the better of what she can realistically manage. She also identifies caring for plants in pots a weakness, along with ensuring that her soil is adequately fed.

Dawn loves variety in her vegetable patch and struggles to identify her favourite crop. "Kale! No, actually it's peas. No, really I love growing carrots. No, really it's garlic!" She loves kale because you can eat it so often throughout the season, even early spring if you let it over-winter. She loves garden carrots "because you can never buy ones that taste as good." Garlic is also at the top of her list because it takes so little effort to yield an amazing crop.

dawn's tip

"Give your plants lots of love and they will give you so much back in return. Get connected with your local seed swap. [It's] an incredible resource of local growing wisdom. Also, start small."

More from Dawn: pp. 47, 61, 175, 186

LLOYD (PEP) HUTCHINSON

Pep was born and raised in Hosmer, a small community on the north side of Fernie. As a young child he helped his grandparents with the potato patch. He and his siblings learned by "watching and getting told how to plant things and look after them."

With his wife Robin, he lives on an acreage. While most of the land is devoted to growing hay for feed, he has a dedicated vegetable patch, as well as a large greenhouse to grow cherry tomatoes, basil, and cucumbers. Pep identifies his favourite part of gardening as "watching the plants grow and seeing all the hard work make it to the table to enjoy." "It's certainly not pullin' weeds," he jokes.

With many family members living nearby, all with a competitive spirit in the garden, Pep is challenged annually to try to grow bigger and better plants. "Some years you just have no luck growing some plants."

Pep loves just about everything he grows, but he really likes to let one or two zucchini go to see how large he can get them. His record to date is 23 lbs!

pep's tip

"Keep your weeds under control…stay on top of it."

More from Pep: pp. 76-77, 113, 186

TERRY NELSON

Terry was born in Port Alberni, BC. At a young age Terry recalls being exposed to gardening, hanging out at the neighbours. His grandparents always had a huge garden where "picking from long rows of strawberries, and shucking tons of peas was a summer norm." He later grew up in Calgary, Alberta, and Sydney, Nova Scotia, before settling in Fernie in 1978.

Terry loves dirt. "I like moving my hands through it, I love the look of a freshly tilled loam, and especially enjoy walking in the wet Elk River silt in my bare feet." While planting and harvesting a garden are both rewarding in their own right, he finds they are second rate to his love for the organic base from which all plants grow.

As far as challenges go, Terry finds "the early fall frost (before September 1st) to be the most intolerable." He has to remind himself the following spring that all the work of planting is really worthwhile.

Terry gets the most enjoyment from a large patch of spinach, which holds off bolting until August. "I like its rich, green colour, and the simplicity of harvesting large bunches, then reducing them to some tasty, sloppy greens."

terry's tip

"Place carrot seeds on top of the tilled earth, then cover them with a thin layer of peat moss. This holds the moisture at the seed level, creating a great germination environment; keeps the planting depth uniform; marks the row really well."

More from Terry: pp. 21, 90, 104, 121, 126, 148-149, 175

HERMA POZNIAK

Herma was born in the early 1930s in Fernie. She has seen a lot of changes over the years in the Elk Valley, but one thing that remains unchanged is her home. She continues to live in the same house she was raised in and is, therefore, very familiar with the garden she tends. In fact, she attributes her garden knowledge to her mother. Herma's intimate knowledge of her patch is tangible. She is able to enjoy potatoes, onions, and carrots, long after the winter snow has settled in the valley.

Herma's favourite times in the garden are when she is planning out her garden and planting it, and again at harvest time. She takes great care to rotate her crops from one year to the next to keep pests to a minimum, and maximize the nutrition in her soil.

Her greatest challenges include deer and couch grass (also known as quackgrass). She sets up a variety of deer deterrents in her garden space but continues to find evidence of their presence on a regular basis.

Herma loves the taste of string beans and lists them as her top vegetable. While she enjoys the taste of home-grown tomatoes, she finds the cold climate of the Elk Valley and the short growing season not adequate to producing a bountiful crop without a greenhouse or some other means to extend the growing season.

herma's tip

"Keep ahead of the weeds."

More from Herma: pp. 14-15, 17, 104-105, 112, 136, 139, 186

ROSETTA RINO

Rosetta was born and grew up in San Giovanni in Fiore, Italy. She immigrated to Canada with her husband in 1978 and settled directly in Fernie. She attributes her knowledge of gardening to her husband, Peppi. They make a great team—Peppi does the design and layout, the digging, and the planting; Rosetta maintains the garden and takes care of the harvest. Together, they have ensured that their vegetable patch gets the greatest amount of sun, which helps maximize their yields.

Rosetta finds gardening both peaceful and rewarding. She says, "you see things growing and then you get the freshest, most organic food possible." Her greatest challenge is getting a sore back when weeding and harvesting in the garden.

Fava beans are Rosetta's favourite crop because they are delicious to eat. Not only are broad beans culturally significant to her, she has found that they grow very well and produce an abundant harvest in the cold climate of the Elk Valley.

rosetta's tip

"Be patient. It is easy to get frustrated and disappointed. Persevere when things don't work out the way you planned or hoped—don't give up."

More from Rosetta: pp. 97, 145, 154-155

VERONICA ROBINSON

Born in Edmonton, Veronica was raised in the small farming community of Edgerton, Alberta. As a child, she started pulling weeds in her garden. She identifies her mother as her mentor. Growing food for sustenance was what she knew. "It's what we lived off of."

In 1995, Veronica moved to the Fernie area and started a garden of her own. She loves many aspects of gardening and struggles to limit the benefits to one. However, both the beautiful aesthetics and the delicious harvest top her list.

Her greatest challenge is the weeds. In her large vegetable patch she finds chickweed particularly rampant. Not one to focus on the negative, she exclaims, "if the weeds get big before you get to them, they are actually easier to pull out." Veronica also finds the chore of ripping a weed out and getting the whole root very satisfying.

Veronica plants a variety of crops and enjoys experimenting with new ideas. She even tried peanuts one year but admits that our short growing season only allowed vigorous plant growth and no harvest. Her all-time favourite choice for home-grown goodness is carrots, simply because they are so easy to grow.

veronica's tip

"Mulching is very important—for moisture retention and to help reduce weeds."

More from Veronica: pp. 45, 48-49, 94-95, 126, 135

VAL RYBAR

Val was born and raised in Czechoslovakia. Not long after she immigrated to Canada in 1970 she attempted her first garden. She recalls, "I had a small plot in Toronto." Two years later she and her husband moved to the Fernie area and ultimately settled in Baynes Lake. As a child she recalls that her mom gardened, but "I didn't pay much attention."

Shortly after arriving in Fernie she met Elizabeth Bachlet. As Val recounts, "she had a wonderful garden and was a huge influence on me. She grew everything in a very large garden. I would observe and learn. We remained good friends until she passed away."

Her favourite part of growing her own food is the spring start. Val starts everything from seed and finds the initial growth very satisfying. Equally, the harvest is rewarding because she gets "so much beautiful stuff and [she] knows exactly how that food has been produced." More challenging is a mild winter, which results in increased insects. Since she doesn't spray Val finds her workload significantly increases because she hand-picks any pests.

val's tips

a. "Every morning, I make a cup of tea and wander through my garden with it to look at everything. If there is anything unusual I note it and tend to it immediately. Staying on top of things is vital.'
b. "Over the winter, I collect all my eggshells, dry them, and come spring, use a hammer to break them into small pieces. I then scatter the pieces throughout the garden to repel slugs, and enrich the soil with calcium."
c. "A fan in my greenhouse keeps aphids away."

More from Val: pp. 43, 62, 92, 107, 142

SUSAN SIM

Susan was born in San Francisco and grew up in rural Northern California, USA. Both sets of grandparents had large gardens and she used to help them as a young child. "I remember my grandfather setting out smudge pots to protect the garden from frost. He also taught me how to irrigate the strawberry patch with a hoe and a series of small ditches." One of her favourite memories is going out into her grandmother's garden on a hot Californian summer day and picking a warm ripe tomato right there.

She moved to the Elk Valley in 1970 and lived on the same property she lovingly tended for 43 years. Over the years Susan created an off-the-grid sustainable oasis with a large vegetable patch, many berry zones, and a medicinal and herb garden. She lived off the land as much as the cold climate afforded, before moving from the area. Susan says, "I love being in the garden listening to birds and the breeze in the trees with my fingers in the soil thinning and weeding."

Susan finds the most challenging aspect of growing food is preparing the beds and then waiting for the seeds to come up. She struggles to pick just one favourite vegetable. She loves all the basics, "like garlic, carrots, peas, and greens because they are both dependable and essential."

susan's tip

"Give your garden lots of compost, rotate your crops, and plant vegetables, herbs, and flowers together to make the most beautiful garden."

More from Susan: pp. 118-119, 139, 166-167

RALPH
STADNICHUK

Born and raised in central Saskatchewan, Ralph spent his childhood on the family farm. He recalls, "back in those days one did not have an option. You either learned to garden or you went hungry." In 1972, Ralph and his wife Margaret moved to British Columbia and settled in Fernie.

A walk by Ralph's garden is a testament to his labour of love. He has set the bar high for the local neighbours and serves as the go-to resource for gardening knowledge and insider tips. Both Ralph and Margaret consider "the ability of tiny seeds to grow and mature right in front of you nothing short of a miracle."

His greatest challenge in the Elk Valley is the weather. Despite years of experience in the cold climate, Ralph is continuously amazed at what the seasons will throw a gardener's way. A walk through his vegetable patch shows an abundant variety of techniques employed to overcome the short growing season. He can also be seen trying out new and often successful designs to overcome pests in the garden.

Ralph cannot pick one single vegetable that he prefers to grow. "Love them all!" he exclaims.

ralph's tip
"Make more compost."

More from Ralph: pp. 29, 46, 69, 115

MARGIE
SUTHERLAND

Born in Vancouver, BC, Margie spent her childhood in Lethbridge and Calgary, Alberta. She started gardening in 1983. "I learned by trial and error. I bought *a lot* of books—there was no Internet back then," she laughs. She still owns the books but finds she references them less and less.

In 1997, Margie, along with her husband Mark, left the city life and relocated to Fernie. She has started more than one garden in the area, having moved homes on several occasions. The result is a superb use of space, strategies that maximize the short growing season, and a prolific harvest. Margie's horticulture background certainly helps.

Her favourite aspect of gardening is eating the results. "Taking my colander out to the garden, filling it up, and then taking a picture of it because it looks so good!" she enthuses. Margie reflects that more space and more time would allow her to enjoy the process even more.

With a greenhouse filled from top to bottom with tomatoes it is easy to guess Margie's favourite crop to grow. She equally enjoys both garlic and raspberries for their flavour, "which is out of this world."

margie's tip
"Start with good soil. I learned the hard way."

More from Margie: pp. 108-109, 144

MADAWNA WIGGINS

Born in Edmonton, Madawna grew up in Spruce Grove, Alberta. She recalls that her mom gardened when she was a child and says she learned some aspects of gardening from her. She moved to Elkford in 1997 but didn't start gardening until 2009. With limited background or experience in growing food she claims she is mostly self-taught, having read a lot of books. She also attended some local workshops.

Madawna's vegetable garden is a wonderful example of what is possible in a cold climate. She says "I really like the challenge of being told you can't garden in Elkford and reaping wonderful rewards. Every year I try something new." As a relatively new gardener, she finds one of her greatest challenges is remembering to start her seeds indoors early enough.

Her favourite crop to grow is cabbages because they grow incredibly well in her climate zone. She utilizes many techniques to extend the growing season including raised beds, hoophouses, and floating row cover. Undoubtedly, as Madawna gains in experience, her garden will only continue to flourish.

madawna's tip
"Just have fun with it. Don't be intimidated. Learn from your mistakes, modify, and just do it!"

More from Madawna: pp. 50-51, 59, 65

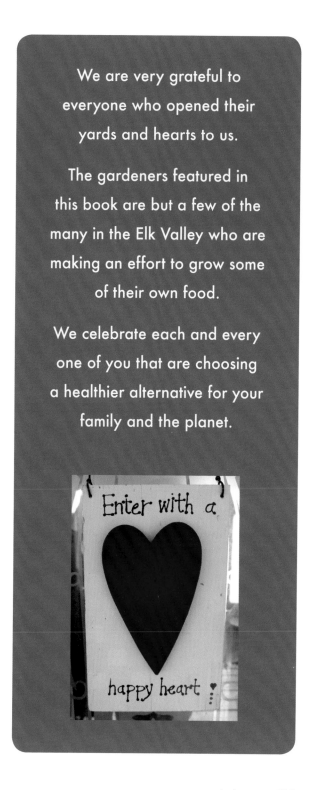

We are very grateful to everyone who opened their yards and hearts to us.

The gardeners featured in this book are but a few of the many in the Elk Valley who are making an effort to grow some of their own food.

We celebrate each and every one of you that are choosing a healthier alternative for your family and the planet.

Enter with a ♥ happy heart

Getting advice from Herma

Dawn & Keya in the EcoGarden

Setting up the exhibit

Amazing tomatoes at Gabriella's

Ella patiently waiting...

Pep shows us his greenhouse

Opening night at The Arts Station

Harvesting arnica at Susan's

HOW IT ALL BEGAN

The idea to write this book began when we decided to find out how local gardeners meet the challenges of growing their own food in the short growing season of the Elk Valley.

We began by "stalking" the back alleys of Fernie, and eventually met gardeners from Jaffray to Elkford. Every where we went, people who supported our research enthusiastically shared their knowledge and backyards with us. We came away with local knowledge and often a few seeds and plants that were happily shared. Passionate gardeners inspired us with their commitment to growing food for themselves, their extended families, and even for surrounding neighbours.

Food security has become a hot topic in the last few years. For many people in Canada, the ability to grow their own food is made all the more challenging by a cold climate and a relatively short growing season. Despite these hurdles, there are many inspiring examples of residents who are growing their own food and enjoying it year-round.

After taking countless photos, interviewing many wonderful gardeners, and completing endless research, we put together a multimedia exhibit called "Down to Earth: Elk Valley Gardens and Their Keepers." It was showcased in May 2010 at The Arts Station in Fernie.

With the ongoing encouragement and support from the Elk Valley communities, this book is the culmination of our efforts. We hope you are inspired, and see the potential of cold-climate vegetable gardening.

thank you!

We are incredibly grateful to Randal Macnair from Oolichan Books who embraced our project from the very beginning. Both he, and his assistant Carolyn Nikodym, guided us with their expertise on writing, designing, and publishing this book.

Also, thank you to Bonny McLardy, Cait Good, Keith Liggett, Keya White, Mike McPhee, and Laura Nelson for generously sharing their experience with us.

Committing to the exhibit gave us the kick-start and ultimate drive to bring this book to fruition. Thanks to Mike Pennock and the Fernie & District Historical Society. Without Mike, the project would not have taken the shape that it did. His complete support and ongoing encouragement was greatly appreciated.

Thank you to the Fernie and District Arts Council and Oz Parsons who endorsed the exhibit. Also thanks to the Columbia Basin Trust and the Columbia Kootenay Cultural Alliance for funding support.

Most of all, we wish to thank the Elk Valley gardeners who welcomed us with open arms and gardens, sharing with us their knowledge and love of gardening. Your enthusiasm was contagious, your tips invaluable, and your kind hearts were always willing to share this amazing valley with us. Thank you—it's been great getting to know you and your gardens.

Finally, thank you to Dave and Ella Fuller, and Steve Lalancette, who supported us and smiled during the many hours of "work" that took us away from home.

RESOURCES
WE LOVE

BOOKS

Alexander, Stephanie. *Kitchen Garden Companion*. London, UK: Quadrille Publishing Limited, 2010.

Biggs, Matthew. *The Complete Book of Vegetables: The Ultimate Guide to Growing, Cooking and Eating Vegetables*. Richmond Hill, ON: Firefly Books Ltd., 2010.

Coleman, Eliot. *Four-Season Harvest: Organic Vegetables From Your Home Garden All Year Long*. White River Junction, VT: Chelsea Green Publishing Company, 1999.

Crocker, Pat. *Preserving: The Canning and Freezing Guide for All Seasons*. New York, NY: William Morrow & Company, 2012.

Damrosch, Barbara. *The Garden Primer: The Completely Revised Gardener's Bible*. New York, NY: Workman Publishing Company, Ltd., 2008.

Denckla, Tanya L.K. *The Gardener's A-Z Guide to Growing Organic Food*. North Adams, MA: Storey Publishing, 2003.

Engeland, Ron L. *Growing Great Garlic: The Definitive Guide For Organic Gardeners and Small Farmers*. Okanogan, WA: Filaree Productions, 1991.

Gordon, Katherine. *The Garden That You Are*. Winlaw, BC: Sono Nis Press, 2007.

Gray, Beverley. *The Boreal Herbal: Wild Food and Medicine Plants of the North: A Guide to Harvesting, Preserving, and Preparing*. Whitehorse, YK: Aroma Borealis Press, 2011.

Hemenway, Toby. *Gaia's Garden: A Guide to Home-Scale Permaculture*. White River Junction, VT: Chelsea Green Publishing Company, 2000.

Herriot, Carolyn. *The Zero-Mile Diet: A Year-Round Guide to Growing Organic Food*. Madeira Park, BC: Harbour Publishing, 2010.

Ivanko, John and Lisa Kivirst. *Rural Rennaissance: Renewing the Quest for a Good Life*. Gabriola Island, BC: New Society Publishers, 2004.

Jabbour, Niki. *The Year-Round Vegetable Gardener*. North Adams, MA: Storey Publishing, 2011.

Kingsolver, Barbara. *Animal, Vegetable, Miracle: A Year of Food Life*. Toronto, ON: Harper Collins Publishers Ltd., 2007.

Martin, Deborah L., and Grace Gershuny, eds. *The Rodale Book of Composting: Easy Methods for Every Garden*. Emmaus, PA: Rodale Press, 1992.

Oster, Maggie. *Herbal Vinegar: Flavored Vinegars, Mustards, Chutneys, Preserves, Conserves, Salsas, Cosmetic Uses, Household Tips*. North Adams, MA: Storey Publishing, 1994.

Ozeki, Ruth. *All Over Creation*. Toronto, ON: Penguin, 2004.

Pollan, Michael. *In Defence of Food: An Eater's Manifesto*. New York, NY: Penguin, 2009.

Smith, Alisa and J.B. Mackinnon. *The 100 Mile Diet: A Year of Local Eating*. Toronto, ON: Random House Canada, 2007.

Solomon, Steve. *Gardening When It Counts: Growing Food in Hard Times*. Gabriola Island, BC: New Society Publishers, 2005.

Spalding, Blake and Jennifer Castle. *With a Measure of Grace: The Story and Recipes of a Small Town Restaurant*. Santa Fe, NM: Provecho Press, 2004.

Tracey, David. *Urban Agriculture: Ideas and Designs for the New Food Revolution*. Gabriola Island, BC: New Society Publishers, 2011.

GREAT ONLINE INFO

The following organizations are wonderful for inspiration and information on gardening, growing vegetables, food security, and so much more. Search for them online.

- David Suzuki Foundation
- Deconstructing Dinner
- Food Secure Canada
- Kootenay Gardening
- Linnaea Farm, Cortes Island, BC
- Mother Earth News
- Seasonal Wisdom

There are also many informative gardening blogs, both long-standing and newly emerging, worth checking out. Staying on top of all that the Internet has to offer is hard to put into print. This is just a starting point.

SEED SOURCES

GE Free BC

Salt Spring Seeds

Seeds of Diversity Canada

Stellar Seeds

USC Canada

West Coast Seeds

William Dam Seeds

INDEX

WELCOME TO THE GARDEN

SNAP

ESPACE PROTÉGÉ POUR LES GRAINES.

MERCI ♥

Missing Creek Garden

BERRIES

THIS IS YOUR LAST CHANCE, BLOOM!